Radical Reflections

Mem Fox

Radical Reflections

Passionate Opinions on Teaching, Learning, and Living

A Harvest Original
Harcourt Brace & Company
San Diego   New York   London

Library of Congress Cataloging-in-Publication Data
Fox, Mem, 1946–
Radical reflections: passionate opinions on teaching, learning, and living/Mem Fox — 1st ed.
p. cm.
ISBN 0-15-607947-X
1. Language arts (Elementary) — United States. 2. Language experience approach in education — United States. I. Title.
LB1576.F665   1993
372.6'0973 — dc20   92-30497

Designed by Lydia D'moch

Printed in the United States of America

First edition

I H G F

For my students,
past, present, and future,
and for Faith Trent, that I might not perish.

Contents

Introduction

At first glance this book will appear to be filled with words. I prefer not to see words but ammunition—ammunition for teachers and parents who are, this minute, engaged in fighting against the still current skills-and-drills mentality in the teaching of language arts; teachers whose belief in whole language is being undermined by a conservative backlash; teachers whose excellent classroom practice cries out for the kind of validation a book such as this might provide.

As I was gathering these articles and presentations and beginning to rewrite them into a coherent volume, I tried to remember I was writing for a wide audience of parents, schoolteachers, would-be teachers, and teachers of teachers, but I kept thinking of a teacher I met recently. I found myself very often writing for her in particular. I don't know her name. She spoke to me after one of my presentations and begged for a copy of my speech.

"I've moved into a new district," she said, "and the principal is giving me no support. I want to continue teaching whole language because I know it works—I proved how well it works in my last school—but my new administrators and fellow teachers are still convinced that skills and drills is the way to go. I have no influence. I'm a lone teacher in a hostile group. A copy of your speech would lend a lot of weight to my pleas for change."

So this book is for her, wherever she is (and for those of her skills-and-drills colleagues who may secretly wish to explore whole language). It's also for all those who find themselves in similar positions of fury and frustration. I hope my nameless friend will be able to use many chapters to provoke positive discussion at faculty meetings; that she will use other chapters to help parents understand what it is she is trying to achieve; and that if she is a parent herself, unhappy about the language teaching in her children's school, she might leave this book in a strategic place, open at the chapter she finds most crucial.

These "radical reflections" grew out of the passionate beliefs I've developed over twenty years about the teaching of language arts at any level. The beliefs in turn grew out of my experiences as a reader and writer, as a teacher of children, as a teacher of teachers, as a parent, and as a woman.

I'm reluctant to choose the single most significant of these experiences, since each has offered me unique insights, but the firsthand wisdom I've been able to glean from being a writer has probably been the most influential factor in determining my theory and practice as a teacher, as the following pages will testify: I believe that "Notes from the Battlefield" is the most important thing I have ever written.

All these ideas were first published in journals or presented as papers at conferences. I am grateful to *Language*

Arts for permission to reprint modified versions of "Notes from the Battlefield," "There's a Coffin in My Office," and "The Fox in Possum's Clothing." Thanks are also due to *The New Advocate* for permission to use a rewritten version of "Once upon a Time There Were Three . . . ," and to *Primary Education* for permission to use "The Paths of Story Lead but to the Graves."

The arrangement of this book is slightly less than haphazard: the first four chapters concentrate on writing and the teaching of writing; the next group of chapters focuses on the teaching of reading, and of language arts in general; and the last few chapters discuss my own writing, in particular writing for children, for which I am probably better known. Having said that, however, each chapter does stand on its own and may be read out of sequence without any confusion.

I hope the faith that fills these pages—my faith in children as learners, my faith in teachers as professionals, and my faith in the power of personal reflection as an aid to better teaching—will help to make the teaching of whole language accessible, rewarding, and above all *possible* for anyone who reads this book.

M.F.
South Australia
December 1992

Radical Reflections

1 Notes from the Battlefield

Toward a Theory of Why People Write

I'm a writer. As such I often see myself as a bloodied and wounded soldier staggering around a battlefield in an attempt to conquer the blank page. As a soldier in the thick of it all, I will try to explain from the battlefield why I write and why others around me write. I'll also try to puzzle out, from the perspective of a war correspondent who stands back and observes, why there are so many deserters out there, refusing to take up their pens and write alongside me. Is it because the wages aren't good enough? Is it because there's nothing worth writing for? Is it because it's only a pretend battle with pretend rewards for pretend winners? We'll see.

Research on how writers write has been illuminating. We choose our own topics, decide our own purposes, target our own audiences, take our time, draft and redraft, talk over our writing with trusted friends and colleagues, and publish our pieces if we're lucky. As a teacher I've applied these writers' conditions in my classes, and I've noticed, of course, a consequent improvement in the effectiveness of my students' writing.

What interests me now is not so much *how* writers write, but *why* we write. What drives us to do it in the first place? And then what makes us want to do it well? If I can find the answers to these questions, I might dare to ask myself another: What are the implications for teachers of writing?

When I was still in the hunting-and-gathering stage of this book, lost in a wilderness of notes, my husband came in to give me a cup of coffee.

"You look really tired," he said.

"I am," I replied, "but I don't mind. I like doing this because it matters." I heard myself say "it matters," and my mind leapt to its feet in a single bound. So that was why I wrote: because it mattered. Was this already an answer to my questions?

I wondered immediately why it mattered. First, I'd been asked to write this book by people whom I liked and admired, so I felt I had to demonstrate my worthiness. I know that an expert is anyone from out of town, but I wanted to prove it to my American readers. It also mattered because of the effect I hoped it might have on me, on you, and on our teaching. I wanted to make a contribution to our thinking, to create a reaction, to cause us all to shift our attitudes somehow, no matter how uncomfortable that shift might be. I wouldn't have dreamed of stumbling into this battlefield and sweating over such an enormous project had I not ached with caring about the insights I wanted to share and the response I was trying to achieve. I had, clearly, a huge investment in this piece of writing.

I used three phrases in the preceding paragraph that I'll be reiterating throughout this chapter. Whenever you read them, I'd be grateful if you'd think of yourself first as a writer and then as a teacher of writing, and ask yourself when you or your students last ached with caring over what you were writing, or wrote because it mattered, or wrote because you had a huge investment in your writing.

Let me begin to focus on caring by way of another story. I teach a compulsory preservice course in language arts to first-year teacher education students. For some years we gave the following assignment: that students should write a letter to the parents of a class of imaginary children explaining the recent innovations and peculiarities in the teaching of reading and writing. It was never brilliantly executed. It was not a real letter; it was an assignment to be marked. It didn't matter to the students; they had only a temporary investment in it, which was to pass the course, and they certainly didn't ache with caring over the response because the audience was imaginary and the response therefore impossible. We don't give that assignment anymore because something occurred that taught us a great deal.

At the time of this assignment, a literacy crank well known in the letter columns of our local press wrote yet another letter to the paper. This time it was in horrified protest at the slovenliness of the "process approach" to the teaching of writing. Three of my students were up in arms about it and decided to write a reply. They huddled together for hours, drafting and arguing. They were in and out of my office all day reading me this sentence and that. I watched them do what T. S. Eliot called engaging in "the intolerable wrestle with words and meanings." They ached with caring because it mattered. They worried about the spelling and punctuation, not wanting the geriatric literacy freak to jump on them and say, "I told you so!" And then, bliss and heaven, it was published! With a huge headline! It was picked up by talk-back radio, and the lines ran hot for half an hour. What a response! What a real reason to write.

At the same time as that real letter was published, the same three students handed in their pretend letters to the parents. I found it hard to believe that students who could on the one hand write so well could on the other write so indifferently. The development of their writing skills in their letter to the paper was palpable, but it didn't flow over into their imaginary letter for the simple reason that "let's pretend" isn't real, doesn't matter, lacks any investment, and won't get a worthwhile response.

If, as this story might imply, language develops only when it is used "for real," then might I suggest that we're currently wasting a lot of time by giving unreal writing tasks in our classrooms: filling-in-the-blanks exercises, copying-chunks-from-encyclopedias exercises, make-believe job applications, "Answer-ten-questions-on-chapter-6" exercises, pretend-letters-to-parents exercises, and so on. You and I don't engage in meaningless writing exercises in real life — we're far too busy doing the real thing. And by doing the real thing we constantly learn how to do the real thing better. Giving unreal writing activities to our students is about as useful as giving occupational therapy for stroke victims to people who are in perfect health.

Among the various drafts of this chapter are sixteen different leads, one of which has currently ended up in my final paragraph because there it's effective: it helps me to sum up and conclude on a powerful note. It would have been crazily unconnected to have kept it at the start of the chapter, but I might have left it there had I not cared about you, my audience, my readers. I wanted you to understand clearly the meanings I was making because they're important to me. The result? I revised. I developed as a writer by developing my writing, which sounds tautologous, but isn't. If the children in our classes don't care about their readers, how can they develop as writers? They can't, because they won't care about what they're writing, and they won't want to revise.

Here's another example of caring being the key to development. It isn't about writing; it's about speaking, but I think you'll see why I want to relate it. In their first semester at college, all my first-year students take a course with me designed to improve their own writing and reading, speaking and listening. For years they have told each other stories in class, recited poems in class, designed and performed choral speaking in class, and read aloud picture books and excerpts from children's novels in class, always to the same audience: their peers. It was merely satisfactory. One year, in a blinding realization of my own stupidity at the meager purpose of these "in-class" assignments, I organized twenty-eight groups of students, about four to six in each group, to visit twenty-eight different real classes in schools close to the college. Their task was to devise and perform a half-hour program of story and song, recited poems and choral poems, picture-book readings, and enthusiastic raves about appropriate novels — anything, in fact, that would enhance their listeners' language development. I called the assignment "Language Alive."

How can I describe the difference in my students' attitude and commitment? It was as if I'd asked them in the past to potter along country lanes in some old Model T Ford and was now surprised to find them screaming down the straight in top gear in the Adelaide Grand Prix. Dreading the imminent and real audience galvanized them into quite a different sort of action: they ached with caring about the response and rehearsed for hours outside class times.

My students' enjoyment of language was extraordinary. I

was moved by how happy they were, astounded by how hard
they worked, and stunned by how much they developed. I
realized with grief that purposeless activities in language arts
are probably the burial grounds of language development and
that coffins can be found in most classrooms, including mine.
It's all so obvious that I feel rather shy about telling these
stories.

I recall my daughter, Chloë, then aged sixteen, being
embattled with an important final-year assignment: a six-
thousand-word reflection on her involvement in the senior
play, *The Effect of Gamma Rays on Man-in-the-Moon Marigolds*.
Every so often she would read bits of her piece to her father
and to me. Being so caught up in my own writing must have
made me a highly unsatisfactory audience. One evening she
read this:

> We realized we had no live rabbit. The problem of
> the rabbit was one that was to hang over us — no!
> Not us, me — for what seemed to be an extremely
> long time. The production began to be divided into
> three distinct periods: B.T.R. (Before the rabbit);
> D.T.R. (During the rabbit); and A.T.R. (After the
> rabbit). I look back on the weeks B.T.R. with consid-
> erable affection.

I smiled and giggled a little. She looked at me balefully
and said, "You're not laughing *enough!*" I was chastened. Her
purpose in reading it had been to make me laugh. I had merely
smiled, which wasn't anywhere good enough for her. I hadn't
noticed how much she'd ached with caring.

When she read sections of the same piece to my husband,

it was to ensure that the content was sufficiently detailed and the writing sufficiently alive. "Is this what they want?" she asked. My husband, Malcolm, was a senior year drama moderator, so from him she was looking for the response of an expert. From me she wanted the response of a clown. We provided these responses, and she was encouraged to continue.

I wonder how often I've given my students an opportunity to write a piece that might have two or more purposes: to make someone laugh, for instance, as well as to fulfill the requirements of a formal assignment. Have I ever given any indication that I enjoy laughing and would be quite happy to roll around on the floor in hysterics while I'm marking their assignments? Do I allow students to hear me laughing over their writing so that they're encouraged to write again? Yes, sometimes I do. I have a loud laugh, and I have often been asked to "shush" when I've disturbed other groups of readers and writers in my class by laughing over someone's writing. But that disturbing laugh is important: it indicates to my students that their writing is effective and therefore worthwhile. My red nose and blotchy eyes are similarly important: "Hey, guess what, guys? Mem really cries if your writing makes her sad." In other words, if they have ached with caring over what they've written, they know I will ache with caring over my response.

One more related story: My position as a published writer in the college means that colleagues view me, erroneously, as an ideal person to talk to about their own writing, although I am acutely aware that *anyone* can respond to a draft in terms of what's confusing, boring, missing, or riveting. Be that as it may, a colleague in environmental education came into my office once, so aching with caring over mining in national

parks that, as he began to read the ending of his first draft of
an open letter to the South Australian minister for the environment, he actually wept. I couldn't believe it! He cared so
deeply about the potential response from the minister and
wanted so much to transform the minister's ideas and to alter
the minister's actions that he was in and out of my office all
day with newly refined drafts. The final letter was tremen-
dously powerful. I wish I could discover what sorts of things
my students care enough about to make them weep with worry
as they try to get their writing right.

Chloë, my drama queen, understands the thrust of my
academic passions as a teacher of the teaching of writing and
is wary of it. She looked up from her own writing one evening and said challengingly, "I'm not enjoying this, you know.
I hate writing." She was attempting to undermine my thesis,
but I didn't kill her. I have other ways of doing battle. Instead, I returned the challenge: "Well, how come you like
writing to J.J. so much? You haven't even met her." J.J. was
her New York pen pal. I had set the trap, and she fell right
into it. This was her reply: "Well, I'm making friends with
her. We like each other. You get to know people through
letters. She writes excellent letters and so do I. We're friends."
Aha! She'd admitted to caring about the relationship.

Mitchell and Taylor (1979), in their pivotal and still relevant paper on the audience/response model for writing, state,
"The writing on the page is not a concrete object but one
portion of a relationship."* All writing, that is, not just letter
writing. I know intellectually that language is an interactive,
social process, but I'm only just beginning to understand what
that means emotionally. My writing, I'm realizing, nearly al-

---

*A listing of major works cited as well as a full bibliography can be found at
the back of this book.

ways has the socially interactive purpose of either creating relationships or ensuring that established relationships continue. I'm being terribly careful about how to behave in the minefield of this first chapter because you, dear reader, matter to me so much. Your possible reaction keeps me nervous and on my toes.

Whenever I write, whether I'm writing a picture book, an entry in my journal, a course handbook for students, or notes for the milkman, there's always someone on the other side, if you like, who sits invisibly watching me write, waiting to read what I've written. The watcher is always important. I've discovered I never write for people of no importance. Showing my writing to that watcher makes me feel weak and vulnerable and almost incapable of battling on. My shakiness over the first draft of this chapter, for example, was so extreme that, while my husband was reading it, I had to leave the room. My only other responder was a woman friend and colleague whom I knew I could trust. I knew she'd still like me even if, in her opinion, I'd written rubbish. Our relationship was, thank God, unassailable.

The more I admire my potential readers, the more carefully I write and the more often I revise. Recently I wrote a student handbook for the second semester, aware, of course, that I was continuing a well-established and hilarious relationship with my students. Of much more importance, however, was the colleague with whom I was about to teach the course. I look up to her. I try to emulate her. I admire her. I wrote the handbook for her, battling over it for weeks. I wanted to bask in the warmth of her praise and gratitude. The handbook was an enormous personal investment in my continuing relationship with her. My writing was currency, and her response was my dividend.

How often are our students able to receive a response

from someone they particularly admire? Some of mine (but never enough of them) admire me. As their teacher I am temporarily important enough for them to ache with caring about what they write for me. Or am I fooling myself? They never write anything for me that isn't also read aloud in class. Is it the response from that wider audience that makes their writing matter? I don't mind what it is as long as someone's response makes them care enough to write effectively, for without that caring how can their writing develop through revision?

For years I had been corresponding with the children from Hallam and Berwick Primary Schools in Victoria. In 1987 we finally met. I arrived armed with photographs of my house, my pets, and my family. We had established such an excellent relationship that the children were sad Malcolm and Chloë couldn't come, too, because they felt they knew them. But Malcolm and Chloë had written them letters, which I read aloud:

Dear Berwick and Hallam kids,

Please keep my mother for as long as you like. I only want her back for Christmas, Easter, and birthdays. Why do you like her so much?

Love,
Chloë

Dear Hallam and Berwickites,

I must have Mem back within twenty-four hours or she'll turn into a toad. Please look after her carefully and return her in one piece.

Much love,
Malcolm

When I arrived home on the following evening, neither Malcolm nor Chloë wanted to hear anything about my trip except the children's response to their letters. Whenever I steered the conversation to more exciting matters, they demanded further, deeper, more fulsome news of the reactions from each of the twenty-six classes. They had written for the purposes of getting a reaction and maintaining a relationship. I was irritated until I realized they were providing me with data for my research into why people write.

I think we tend to forget about this element of relationships when we teach writing. Are we aware of how much our students dread having their writing knocked back? Do we trample on their vulnerability when they limp in, unarmed, from the battlefield? Do we remember how much the caring over their writing is often also an aching to make friends, with us and with their peers? It's hard to keep in mind the painful wounds of battle and the importance of friendship unless you've been wounded yourself. Teachers of writing who have been soldiers themselves, engaged in a writing battle, must be able to empathize more closely with the comrades in their classrooms than teachers who are merely war correspondents at the hotel bar, as it were, watching the battle from a safe distance, declining to get in there themselves and write.

When the refreshing ideas of Donald Graves swept through our writing classes in the early eighties, I believed that the ultimate purpose in writing was to be published. Since then I have become a published writer myself, and I realize how wrong I was. It's what happens beyond publishing that's important: it's the response to my work that matters. *Wilfrid Gordon McDonald Partridge* has been published in both England and the United States. In America it is loved and I'm feted for it. In England no one seems to know about it, except my sister, and I get no response, so I become despondent and wonder why I ever bothered to write it. Then I come home again, and a colleague comes into my office and sobs hysterically for two hours. She's just read the book and is overcome because her own mother has Alzheimer's disease. It's a wonderful response.

Yet another story! When I left Australia at the age of six months, I was Miss Partridge. When I came back in 1970, I was Mrs. Fox. Friends of my parents called Mr. and Mrs. Bunney (yes, really!) looked after us in those first few months and helped us to settle in. Bronte Bunney later employed me, and we worked together at the college for fifteen years, often laughing over the ridiculousness of our surnames. When Bronte retired, I wrote him a tiny book called *The Bunney and the Fox*. It was published. I "published" it myself. I couldn't find him on that last Friday afternoon, and I longed to so I could watch his response as he read the book. I was desperate. I'd heard he'd be clearing out his office on Saturday morning. I went there. He wasn't. I drove to his house. He was out. I was ready to scream. In the end I left it by his front door, knowing gloomily that I'd never see his response; I'd just have to wait to hear it. Here's the book:

The Bunney and the Fox

Once upon a time there lived a Partridge and a Bunney. The Bunney was beautiful and brilliant but never bashful. And he was always busy. One day, far across the world, the Partridge turned into a Fox. And not long afterwards she traveled to the place where the Bunney had his home. For a long time the Bunney and the Fox worked happily side by side. Not much changed except that besides being beautiful and brilliant the Bunney was also very kind to the Fox. He encouraged her greatly and said nice things to her face and behind her back. And the Fox became so used to having the dear Bunney around that when the Bunney went away — as indeed he did — she wondered, with a lump in her throat, whether she really could live happily, ever after.

It's hard to imagine my students ever chasing anyone around the countryside in a desperate craving for a response to their writing, but that is my goal.

There are responses and then there are responses, some of which are financial. I wrote *Sail Away* partly to make money. I had earned such a sum from *Possum Magic* that I had been continually running after myself in order to pay the estimated tax. In fact, for a long time after *Possum Magic* I labored under the illusion that the financial benefits of writing were among my purposes for putting pen to paper. I've come to discover that this isn't really the case.

Several years ago I wrote a long and passionate newspaper article on why we sent our precious only child to the local state high school instead of to a private one. I was paid for this article in March. For some reason it was never published. Every Sunday morning I would stagger bleary-eyed down the drive in my battered blue dressing gown and rip open the paper in a fever of anticipation. Nothing! I realized two things: first, I wanted to be published more than I wanted to be paid. Second, it was the reaction to my piece that I longed for. Publication was merely the first hurdle along the road to response.

Nevertheless, knowing that cash can be a tremendous incentive, I did suggest at a crowded workshop at Columbia

University Teachers' College that we pay children for what they write before we put their pieces into a class library. Wouldn't you think that a writing seminar in New York, of all places, would be full of hustlers? But no! Lucy Calkins was speechless. Was it with horror? And Shelley Harwayne was in hysterics. In spite of that, I bravely paid eleven of my students for the privilege of publishing their writing in a booklet called "Picking Up the Pieces," which was designed to demonstrate to other students what I believe effective writing to be. If royalties are a postpublication response that matters enough to make my students ache with caring, I think they're worth considering, outrageous and grubby though the idea may seem at this moment. If it's good enough for real writers, why isn't it good enough for real student writers?

I think it might safely be said that in general people don't expect to write much after they've left school, except when it's absolutely necessary — as a tool, in letter writing for instance, or when it's part of their work. In short, it's seen as a chore. The view that writing might be fun, or amusing, or relaxing is not, I imagine, widely held, and we teachers must be to blame for that.

During the writing of this chapter, a letter arrived from one of my publishers, exhorting me to write a poem for their forthcoming volume for children called *Vile Verse*. I put the letter away. But when the going got tough, the tough got going. In the same way that one searches for handkerchiefs to iron when the strain of ironing shirts becomes too much, I began to work on a poem, as a form of relaxation. I remembered with delight the groans of disgust from kids who'd heard my first putrid poem, "The Teacher's Cold," and set to with energy to write the following:

Sweet Samantha, Unrefined

When sweet Samantha eats her food
She is exceptionally rude:
Her mouth is always open wide
So you can see the view inside.
It's not a pretty sight, my friends,
To see how Sammy's dinner ends—
Across her tongue the pieces float
Around her teeth, towards her throat:
You almost vomit while she chews
And tells you all the latest news!
It's terrible when fish and chips
Come shooting forth between her lips
Or when she's eating lamingtons
And bits of coconut grow wings
And catch you right between the eyes—
Your stomach soon begins to rise!
But scrambled egg is quite the worst:
It looks as though her cheeks will burst
With all the stuff which fills her mouth
From east to west and north to south.
My dears, it is a frightful sight
When sweet Samantha takes a bite,
So my advice is stand well clear
Especially when she starts to cheer,
And do make sure that you have dined
Before, Samantha, unrefined,
Attacks her stew and starts to chew
And sprays her food all over you.

As I wrote that very vile verse, I realized that my purposes for writing anything never come in ones but always in twos and threes or more. First, I wrote it because it was fun. I also wrote it for Chloë because I knew it would disgust her and that we'd laugh over it together, thereby building on our continuing relationship. I also wrote it for Malcolm, who was tapping away on a calculator, looking very despondent over our finances. I knew it would cheer him up, not only because it was so revolting but also because it would earn a dollar a line if it were published, thereby enabling him to pay at least $28 off the Visa bill. And finally, I wrote it for the children of Australia as an antidote to the honeyed sweetness of my *Possum Magic* and *Hattie and the Fox*.

I hadn't realized how often I wrote for fun until Malcolm read the first draft of this chapter and said, "I'm amazed that you haven't explained how writing is central to your life. It fascinates you. It rewards you. It fatigues you. Nowhere have you actually said you can't live without writing." Can't live without writing? Had I heard correctly? I loathe writing! It's so easy to do badly and so difficult to do well that I quail before each new writing task. I particularly detest the battle to produce a picture-book story in less than 750 words. Of course I can live without writing — or can I?

One day when I was out shopping I met the deputy principal from Chloë's primary school. She had, that very week, come across a letter I'd written back in 1977 about Chloë's being absent from school. She'd kept it because it had made her laugh. Goodness knows which letter it was; I'd written so many for one reason or another. Chloë's tenth-grade math teacher has a whole file of them, each attempting to be funnier than the last to distract his attention from her dismal performance and incomplete homework. It's true I can't live without writing. Every time the chance to write arises, whether it's to the window cleaner about leaving the dogs in the back

garden, not in the house, or to the lawyer about the prolifer-
ation of *Possum Magic* products and its ramifications, my aim
is to enjoy myself. I love imagining the reader reading what
I've written because, I suppose, I've had such terrific responses in the past. I just can't resist messing around with
writing.

I can't not try because my sense of audience is so strong.
It might result from having trained as an actress for three
years in the Stanislavski tradition: I can see and hear my
imagined readers very clearly. I can't even sign a birthday
greeting without going into battle with the blank side of the
card. A feminist bookshop in Adelaide was having its fifth
birthday, so I signed a card but couldn't seal it. I stood pon-
dering in the post office. The bookshop is called The Murphy
Sisters. What could I write? All I could think of was, "The
boy stood on the burning deck. . . ." The boy? For a feminist bookshop? Suddenly it came:

The girl stood on the burning deck
Her feet were full of blisters
She could not move —
Her head was in
A book from Murphy Sisters.

What does all this have to do with the teaching of writing? First, I wonder how often we demonstrate our crazy,
private note writing to our students? It's probably not much
of an option in their lives because they don't know that it's
possible, that such fun exists, and that it's rewarding for its
own sake, let alone for the glorious responses it creates. I'm
wrong, of course. They do know. What about all those underground notes students write to each other in class? Why

can't we legitimize it? Wouldn't it make our classrooms come alive if kids giggled and shrieked in the open about writing that was written in the open instead of underground?

Second, isn't it incredible how often writing means writing stories? I can't stand writing stories. Honestly! I never write them from my imagination — only when an idea from life or books jumps into my head, not out of it. I have about four ideas a year, and I'm a proficient, professional, published writer, yet we ask children to write story after story. What's wrong with letters, for instance? Clarity, voice, power, and control are much more easily developed through letter writing because, perhaps, the audience is so clearly defined and will, if all goes well, respond. Writing for fun is not just for fun — it's for the long-term, conspicuous development of the craft itself.

Within the fun of writing there is also power. It seems to me that the most delicate transactions are best dealt with through a sort of self-effacing humor that makes one's point without causing offense. But do we ever communicate the possibility of this kind of writing to our students so that they might become similarly empowered in their own lives? I shared the following letter with my students to demonstrate the kind of writing I have used beyond my schooling. It was to the architect of our home extensions, toward the end of the building project:

Dear Brian,

Here I am, home again, and eager to bring The Extension Situation to a close. The State Bank is satisfied with the work and will pay the builder as soon as we indicate in writing that we are similarly satisfied. A few things still require attention, however.

1. There are still no handles on the drawers in my office. This is, as you can imagine, an extreme hazard to my nails!

2. The toilet seat is so badly positioned that it will not stay up. I fear the intimate damage this may cause any male guest . . .

3. The bricks in the patio have not been replaced and, as it is unlikely that we shall excavate for buried treasure in the near future, I would like them replaced as soon as possible.

4. Although we do not see eye to eye with our neighbor (he is very short), I would be unhappy to see him killed by falling bricks when he leans over the fence to gasp in admiration at our extensions. The brick wall separating our properties could, at present, be pushed over by a child. The damage to the wall was caused during the initial excavations. Early rectification of this danger would be appreciated.

5. Otherwise the place is a perfection of taste and convenience — thank you! I love it.

The State Bank mentioned that the builder was expecting all the rest of the money. I was puzzled because I understood that we would save approximately $2,000 by not having a retaining wall built. I have exquisitely good eyesight and search though I might, I cannot find a retaining wall! I hope that you can clarify this situation. I am a writer, not a mathematician.

With happy thanks,
Mem Fox

I am not at all surprised, considering the purpose of this letter, that Mitchell and Taylor (1979) understand writing to be "a means of acting upon a receiver. Its success will be judged by the audience's reaction: 'good' translates into 'effective,' 'bad' into 'ineffective.' Instead of a product, we are studying an interaction, a dynamic relationship with all the complexities that involves" (p. 250). My letter to the architect was framed and now hangs on his office wall among his diplomas. And the extensions were completed to our entire satisfaction. The letter was effective.

I'm anxious about the power, or lack of it, in school writing. Power is about being able to craft a piece of writing so effectively that its purpose is achieved. *Craft* means understanding the nature and importance of leads and endings; of showing, not telling; of sharpening and tightening; of structure and focus; of purpose and audience; and of the conventions. *Craft* means being able to put those understandings into practice. *Craft* means struggling in that battlefield between the brain and the hand until the best possible draft is achieved. Children won't learn how to be powerful by writing identical letters to Mem Fox, as so often happens, alas. So depressing!

I regularly use the power of my own writing to manipulate the world into granting my wishes. For example, I remember applying for and receiving vast funding to attend a conference in New Zealand at which I wasn't even presenting a paper. The committee concerned had collapsed into unwilling giggles over my application and, hey presto, there was my air ticket! And best of all, in 1986 I jumped over five incremental steps in my promotion to senior lecturer, a feat so daring I wouldn't have attempted it had I not had confidence in my own power to write a sufficiently stunning application.

Such power doesn't come from nowhere. It comes from practicing writing for real reasons. It comes from having read powerful writing. It comes from having been taught, and I mean taught, the basic skills of spelling and punctuation in the context of real writing events. Those who write well have more power and therefore have more control over their lives. It seems to me to be a supreme arrogance on our part as teachers not to see that the granting of this power to our children is politically and socially essential. In the end they must be able to spell and punctuate; they're powerless without those skills. Their power won't come about without practice, and the practice can't come about without purpose. The hardest thing for me as a teacher is discovering purposes that will excite my students to such an extent that they'll risk the trauma of the writing battle. It's hard, but it mustn't be impossible, for their sakes.

I haven't given much thought to it yet, but I have more than a hunch that power in writing actually deteriorates the further ahead children travel in their schooling. Many of my teacher education students, after twelve years at school, come to me helpless and fearful as writers, detesting it in the main, believing that they can't write because they have nothing to say because they haven't cared about saying anything because it hasn't mattered because there's been no real investment for so long. How I wish we could change this situation. We must give power to our people.

Before I'm carried from this battlefield on a stretcher, let me rapidly summarize my notes. The insights I have as to why I write make me believe that as a teacher I must try to:

- Help students to care about writing by making it real.
- Give my students opportunities for real responses from people they admire.
- Create situations in which students always own the investment in their writing.

- Be sensitive to the social nature of writing, and the vulnerability of writers.
- Demonstrate and encourage writing for fun and huge enjoyment and power.
- Respond after publication as well as before.
- Help to develop powerful writing so that my students can control their own lives.

In my last will and testament I'd like to leave you this theory: Children develop language through interaction, not action. They learn to talk by talking to someone who responds. They must therefore learn to write by writing to someone who responds. It's not a new theory, but it's one I keep forgetting even though it's so clear and simple. Please keep it somewhere safe.

I don't mind if you, dear reader, forget most of what I have written in this chapter except for one phrase: "to ache with caring." If we as teachers ache with caring it will, perhaps, be possible for us to create classroom communities within school communities in which writing matters because it's done for real reasons by real writers who ache with caring for a real response.

My hope is that through the grimy windows of my particularity we've been able to peer into a more generalized world — that we can now move into that world as agents of change so that our students write more, write more often, write more effectively, and write with greater willingness and enjoyment. I wish we could change the world by creating powerful writers for forever instead of just indifferent writers for school.

2 | There's a Coffin in My Office

I'm not a funeral director, but it's true: there's a coffin in my office. Neither am I a hypochondriac, but there's a large bottle of pills on my filing cabinet. In mid-November 1989, there was a 1990 calendar hanging on my office wall. I've never been a prison officer, but I once had criminal records littering my desk. And in spite of the fact that it's been nearly twenty years since I taught first grade, a line of bright yellow cardboard ducks marches across my bulletin board. These and many other items clutter my work space. It's chaos.

This chapter, and the chaos in my office, explain in part how I teach as a professor of language arts in a university setting — how I put into practice the ideas I expressed in the previous chapter.

The treasures I've described are end-of-semester assignments from two hundred first-year teacher education students who had just completed a compulsory introductory course in the teaching of language arts. They — the students — were as various as their assignments. Their ages stretched from seventeen to forty-two. Some were still children. Others had children. Some played the flute. Others played football. A few played with fire. Language arts, in most cases, was not central to their lives, yet they stepped with pride into my office to deliver a concrete metaphor that illuminated language arts in a unique fashion, and I was so excited I had gooseflesh in spite of the intense summer heat.

What are these metaphors? At the end of the course our students present two assignments. The first is a "Dream Piece," in which we ask them to demonstrate as creatively as possible that they have understood the major theories and practices to which they have been exposed for the past fourteen weeks. From past experience we know that the act of transferring newly learned ideas into a concrete symbol demands a high level of intellectual reflection and entails a much deeper engagement with theory than appears to be the case with more traditional end-of-term papers. The second assignment is a "Dream Folder," in which the students gather academic articles, poems, stories, booklists, information on children's writers, practical ideas for the classroom, and any other material they think might be useful in their teaching of language arts.

Our final workshop is a grand occasion of celebration and revision as the students present their Dream Pieces to the class — pieces like Shannon's coffin, for instance. Inside is a doll. A child. Dead, of course. Malnourished in the language arts desert and starved of good books, according to the death certificate. Overdosed on the evil of worksheets, which are not real writing for real responses from real people. Sickened to death by the lifeless prose of basal readers, and so on. R.I.P.

The pills in the bottle are part of Mark's Dream Piece. They'd been prescribed for a book hater who had been confined to a psychiatric institution after having been caught burning down libraries. According to Mark's persuasive fiction, sad experiences in language arts caused this child to loathe books and reading as well as writing. However, under the guidance of Dr. Fox and Dr. Wilkinson (of whom more anon), the child's treatment consisted of being encouraged to write using invented spelling on any topic, which would be responded to personally by each doctor in turn. And the pills? Well, they were to be administered as required. In the final class, as he was presenting his Dream Piece, Mark passed around the bottle and told us all to take a pill and pull it apart. It was in capsule form. Tightly rolled in each tiny container was the name of a terrific book for kids.

Like Mark's pills, Kerry's criminal records look authentic: they're written on forms used in real prisons. Each form has a "photo" on it — a picture cut from a magazine. Name, age, height, and weight are recorded. In two major columns are (1) the offense and (2) the sentence. There are eight prisoners' files; here's my favorite:

Offence: Andrew Adam Schultz was seen committing a Language Arts major crime on May 21st, 1989, by the teacher aid. A girl in Andrew's class was having difficulty with a word, so she had a go and made an approximation of it. Andrew not only scribbled all over it in a red pen and made fun of the child, but he also made her stay in for the whole of her playtime to write the correct word over and over again. The teacher aid reported the crime immediately, and Andrew was arrested within the hour.

Sentence: Andrew Adam Schultz is sentenced to three years at the Sturt College of Advanced Education. He is to repeat the Language Arts course each year,

attending all available lectures, workshops, and tutorials. It is hoped that Andrew will learn that approximation in writing is merely a beginning and that
children are not expected to have adult competence.

Would that I had the dictatorial power of this arresting
officer. I think I'd arrest the arrogant publishers first — those
who purport, insultingly, to be able to produce "teacher-proof"
ditto sheets. I'd boil those big, bad publishing wolves in oil
and make sure they had to spend the rest of their lives engaged in the hell of meaningless writing activities.

Above the mess of these grim criminal records hangs Tash's
outrageous calendar for 1990. It's real. Every date falls on the
right day — even Easter and Christmas are correctly placed.
The week of my birthday in early March is, I notice, desig-
nated as "Burn the Basals Week." October 15 is the beginning of "Paper Plane Week" — a week in which it is suggested
that all ditto sheets be made into paper planes since that's all
they are good for. Said Tash, "If they don't exist for real-life
writers, why should they exist in the classroom?" She also
said I wasn't allowed to keep the calendar. "It's not an assignment, Mem! It's a real and precious piece of writing for a real
and useful purpose, Mem!" However, she weakened and I still
have it on my wall.

Alongside the calendar, Susie's adorable bright yellow ducks
beg for attention, one after the other. Each has a verse attached to its wings. The tune for the verses is clearly the same
as the tune for "Five Little Ducks," except that this time there
are eight:

Eight little ducks went out one day,
Down to the library, not far away.

Mother Duck said, "Quack, quack, quack, quack,"
But only seven little ducks came back.
(The other little duck was deeply immersed in
    reading) . . .
Three little ducks went out one day
Reading poems to their fiancees.
Mother Duck said, "Quack, quack, quack, quack,"
But only two little ducks came back.
(The other little duck got the response
    he wanted) . . .

When this assignment was presented in class, we all sang along, in hysterics over the song and jubilant that the end of the year was upon us. The sense of community was strong. Lively use of language occurred in a real social context, which provided a worthwhile incentive for students to reflect on their learning and to write as effectively as possible. It also provided the opportunity for a real response. Within this celebration of people's unique efforts was a demonstration of the academic and emotional power available to anyone who genuinely cares about making meaning through words.

These assignments and their ramifications don't occur without a lot of groundwork, so let me explain the tone, attitudes, and methods that pervade our classes.

I share the teaching of this course in a lecture/workshop/ tutorial system with three other professors. Although we're deeply serious about teaching and learning, we're rarely serious in the act of teaching. We cavort through our classes, exposing our students to a variety of language experiences, many of them lighthearted, in order to demonstrate the vivacity and potential of reading and writing, speaking and listening. We try to use language energetically to amuse and enthuse. We hope we're successfully modeling the fact that language is a vital tool that can be employed with power and enjoyment for many different purposes.

Our first lecture begins in darkness. Lyn and I — Lyn Wilkinson is one of my wilder colleagues — light three candles. For a rare moment we look as demure as angels, heads bowed. A hush falls over the packed lecture theatre. Softly we begin to read a story together, dividing the lines chorally:

> Once upon a time, / but not very long ago, / deep in the corridors of Sturt College / there lived two lecturers. / They loved language arts / and longed to pass on their knowledge / and ideas, / their hopes / and their passions / to their beloved students. / "How shall we capture their hearts and minds?" / said one to the other. "More's to the point," / said the second, / "how shall we capture their attention in the first place?" / They decided to begin in darkness with three lighted candles, / and, lo! the attention of the students was caught.

Of course the attention is caught. The students grin and groan and roll their eyes, dreading the inevitability of similar weak jokes throughout the lecture.

Our aim with every offbeat activity is to model a genre, to model correct English, to model enjoyment, and to model a range of emotional possibilities in language arts. We know that dullness and perceived irrelevance have punctuated much of our students' learning of English in high school; we also know that those who have been turned off have to be turned back on, so we do our utmost to teach divertingly and divergently.

In a subsequent lecture, in order to make the point that the language environment has an enormous effect on children's language development, I bring in buckets of water into which I plunge naked dolls to demonstrate the "immersion" factor. It's crassly obvious, but it grabs attention, enabling me to teach through the splashes and the laughs.

- If the water is Italian, will this child learn English? No! She'll learn Italian!
- If the water is a home without books, will this child be an avid reader? No! He'll be an avid watcher of television!
- If the water is a classroom in which the teacher bathes this child in good literature by reading aloud every day, will the child's reading and writing develop in leaps and bounds? Yes!

By attempting to be creative ourselves as teachers and users of language, we give our students not only a demonstration of teaching options but also the permission to use those creative options themselves. We demonstrate that effective learning and teaching are rarely based on chalk-and-talk.

One of the most obvious effects of this modeling is that our students are daring to be more thoughtful and more bizarre in tutorial presentations. A tutorial in our system is an hour-long session led entirely by a student on any topic relevant to language arts. The professors join in as ordinary members of the class. In a tutorial on assessment in which hot discussion took place over the effectiveness of gold stars or smiley stamps on children's writing (conclusion: negative), our student leader told us to rewrite the song "Twinkle, Twinkle, Little Star" to explain our philosophical stance on the issue. Debate then continued on a variety of response and evaluation procedures. At the end of the tutorial we were asked to lie on the floor and put our feet high up on the wall. The student in charge of the tutorial held up a large sign that said ASSESSMENT.

"Can you all see that?" he asked.

"Yes!" we replied, even though we were looking at it upside down.

"Good," he said. "You've now looked at assessment from a different perspective!"

The medium and the message of this tutorial provided such a buzz that its contents came up in discussion again and again throughout the semester.

We often use singing to teach major points in our lectures. For example, in order to express my passionate belief that writers don't improve their craft unless they have a real purpose, a real audience, and a real investment in their writing, I rewrote two well-known songs, the first of which began like this:

> Pack an investment in your old kit bag,
> And smile! Smile! Smile!

Because I'm not Maria Callas, I don't sing by myself. We all sing together, with more volume and gusto than tune. The lecture ends with this:

> Where has all the purpose gone,
> Long time passing?
> Where has all the purpose gone,
> Long time ago?
> Where has all the purpose gone?
> Gone from classrooms every one.

When will we ever learn?
When will we ever learn?

The melody lingers in the lecture room as the students file out, and it lingers in their minds — we hope — more than formal instruction might.

One of the most exciting offshoots of this course is the influence of our students' writing on our own writing-in-response. Their Dream Pieces manipulate us into having fun with a variety of outlandish genres that don't normally present themselves in our academic lives. One example, a Dream Piece by Donna, had been written and presented to look and sound like the Bible. Inside, after a dedication page that said, "God bless the great teachers," were fourteen commandments, each of which was followed by lesser commandments. For example:

12. Thou Shalt Develop Real Writers

- Good writers steal: fill the children's storehouse's [*sic*] with good literature
- Demonstrate writing
- Make writing real
- Find real audiences
- Allow time, and choice of topic, etc.

I could have responded formally, but the nature of Donna's assignment encouraged me to have fun with language in the same way:

Donna:
  Thou hast filled the commandments of thy noble
leader as it was said in the beginning:

- *that thou shouldst be as creative as possible*
- *that thou shouldst include those theories and practices which thou hast learned this semester*
- *that thou shouldst make clear thine own personal understandings*
- *that thou shouldst provide thyself with an easy-to-read resumé of the main ideas explored with thy noble leader and thine even more noble compatriots this semester*
- *that thou shouldst be correct at all times in thy presentation of content, spelling, grammar, and punctuation (only one error! Thou didst put an apostrophe on a plural, thou mighty sinner: "storehouses" doesn't need an apostrophe: nothing belongs, nothing is left out.)*
- *that thou shouldst reach for the stars and fulfil the high expectations of thyself as well as those of thy noble leader.*

> *In grateful thanks*
> *for what I have received.*
> *Ah, Mem! xxx*

Because I love messing about with words, I'm thrilled when I see my students reveling in language, too. I always hope that their assignments will show evidence of enjoyment, as well as a clear grasp of academic content. I'm rarely disappointed. Inside one Dream Folder I was assaulted by this verse:

Dear Mem,
> *Here is the start of my precious Dream Folder*
> *Which will forever increase as I grow older.*
> *Please look after it as if it were your own*
> *Or I will come after you, wielding a stone!*

> *Thanks, Mem.*
> *Justin*

Faced with such artistic provocation, I had to reply in kind:

Justin, my dearest, my darling young man —
I'll take as much care as I possibly can.
It's true that your folder is totally brilliant,
And you've survived all my classes!
My God! How resilient!

> *Much love,*
> *Mem*

I realize with elation that I'm no longer guiding my students down a one-way street of language. No longer am I the lonely only one who directs writers to "have a go." No longer am I the only one who shows the way toward different genres and strategies, products and processes. Through their assignments my students have taken control, and I'm aware that they're now guiding me. The power base has shifted. We're a community of writers, leading each other from one written destination to another. How humbled I am. And how proud.

The divergent nature of Justin's assignment and those of his friends means that marking takes on a new dimension. That dreaded task, which used to make me so gloomy, has been replaced by celebration after celebration. I love responding to my students' intriguing ideas; their work is suddenly a pleasure to read.

We're often anxious about the amount of fun we have as we revel in language arts with our students. "If we're all having such a good time," we ask ourselves, "can they really be learning those deep theories that are the necessary basis for good practice?" Immediately after our course comes the long summer vacation. Will the level of recall at the beginning of our students' second year reveal that we have failed as teachers? Happily, in most cases, our doubts are put to rest. The lecturers who teach language arts to second-year students stop us in the corridors or accost us at coffee time with throwaway remarks like these: "They know so much!" "They're really keen on language arts, aren't they?" "What did you do to them? They love writing!"

We know intellectually that we should trust our students to learn — after all, that's what we preach — but we're only human, so we tremble with doubt from time to time about what we're doing. It's a tremendous relief, therefore, to have our trust justified year after year.

As I continue to reflect on every aspect of our course, I'm starting to understand that the coffin in my office holds much more than a dead doll. Through the excitement and enlightenment of our students, we are burying past mistakes in the teaching of English. Inside the coffin, alongside the doll in neat metaphorical rows, lie the causes of her death: dead ideas, dead theories, and dead practices. I'm a little nervous that some of this decay might escape and begin to contaminate me, so I've sealed the coffin tightly and placed it just so, under my desk where it doubles nicely as a footstool. Death, be not proud! In my world, among my students, language arts is, for the time being, alive and well and living down under.

3 | The Paths of Story Lead But to the Graves

This chapter reiterates, in a shorter form, some of the themes of chapter 1. Its particular focus, however, is a nuts-and-bolts analysis of the meaning of "process writing," beginning with the proposition that if we are so foolish as to dare to teach writing without ever writing ourselves, we are treading with arrogance on shaky ground. This proposition was one of the foundations for the course I described in chapter 2: we wanted our students to have grass-roots experiences of *being writers* before they set foot inside classrooms and attempted to become teachers of writing.

We know that Donald Graves has had a profound influence on the teaching of writing. His message has been this: "Look at real writers. Observe their needs. Discover the process they go through and the reasons why they write. Then re-create those conditions in your own classrooms." But we tend not to *discover* the writing process — we only read about it and imagine that's good enough. It isn't. Unless we experience *firsthand* the agonies and ecstasies of writing, we may fast discredit this new method by engaging in inept and inappropriate classroom practice.

I am a real writer at this exact moment, struggling to write. In exploring my process as I write, I hope to illustrate the kinds of learning that are taking place and how that learning might make me a better teacher of writing than one who never puts pen to paper other than to fulfill his or her professional obligations.

The first consideration in writing or teaching writing is **choice of topic.** Real writers choose their own topic; therefore, children should be allowed to do the same. I chose the topic for this chapter. When I suggested it to the editor she didn't say, "No, you can't write about that. Write about this." Instead she showed interest in what I had to say. I was encouraged. Eager to start.

There are times, however, when I can't choose my own topic. When I was asked once to write an article on storytelling, I collapsed in a heap and whimpered, "But I haven't got anything fresh to say. Tell me what to write. Give me a title." The editor obliged. I was encouraged. Eager to start! So, from personal experience, I have learned that I usually like to choose my own topic, but not always. It has made me more flexible with my own students. I no longer feel guilty when I chat with struggling writers and suggest what they might write about. I've been there; I know how they feel.

The second essential ingredient in the magic is **purpose** — a real purpose. My purpose, as a real writer, writing a real chapter for a real book, is to persuade teachers of writing to write. I'm not writing because it's my set time of day to engage in writing. I'm writing because I'm anxious: I'm fearful that these new ideas for the development of literacy will be killed and buried by a bunch of grave-digging nonwriters. My purpose is not to write a story, thank heavens! I loathe writing stories. The plot nearly kills me. *Possum Magic* took five years to perfect, and the book that followed, *Wilfrid Gordon McDonald Partridge*, was such torture to write that I thought I'd never write again.

Yet what do we see in the loveliest and most advanced Graves-type writing classrooms? Children stuck in a story-writing rut. Kids who can't think of a plot feel reluctant to write, no matter how encouraging the general atmosphere. Being a writer has helped me understand that story writing is one of the most difficult of all the writing acts. I now tap into kids' concerns and their memories, suggesting "I care about . . ." pieces and "I remember . . ." pieces instead of burdening them with a task that makes me quail.

Another sadness I've come across in relation to story writing is that kids who can't draw hate writing. What on earth, you may ask, has the ability to draw got to do with the willingness to write? It's my belief that too much emphasis is put on kids' illustrating their own writing. Real writers who can't paint don't illustrate their own stories. Roald Dahl had Quentin Blake. I have Julie Vivas, without whom my first two books would never have seen the light of day. I can't draw at all, so my heart bled in sympathy for the little writer who said, "I hate writing because of the pictures after." I know how she feels because I do write and I don't illustrate. How many nonillustrating nonwriters could sympathize with that child?

The next element of process writing to be explored is **audience.** I have an audience for this book — my editor, at least, if no one else. Although I care deeply about it, I wouldn't have dreamed of writing it had I thought that no one would

read it and find it interesting, irritating, useful, old hat, pro-
vocative, or something. No one writes for no one to read.
Not even journal writers (in their heart of hearts) write just
for themselves-in-private.

I have a group of friends who would read this chapter,
out of loyalty if nothing else, but I write for them all the time.
Besides, they're writers, too, so they would agree with my
theme. I needed a new audience this time, which makes me
realize that often children do, too. The class is fine as audience for a while, but now that I know, as a writer, how excited
I am by the prospect of a fresh group of potential readers I
will struggle to find new audiences for my class: another class,
someone's grandmother, the editor of a newspaper, politi-
cians, TV stations, and so on.

How much time should I allow my students to spend on
each piece of writing? Real writers need the **time** they need —
they're all individuals with different ways of working. I need
a deadline, so I bravely suggested to my editor that I would
do the final edit on this book within four weeks. As I write,
that was three weeks ago. I've been working flat out for the
last five days. I should have organized my time better — I should
have started long ago, but even niggling guilt wasn't spur
enough. It's the "next week" element that catapults me into
action. We ought to know our kids well enough to push the
ones who need pushing and to leave alone the ones we can
trust. I can't be trusted.

However, sometimes a deadline kills my creativity entirely. A sequel to *Possum Magic* was once asked for, by such-
and-such a date. I tried. I tried again. Nothing happened. It
was like trying to squeeze toothpaste out of an empty tube.
All the drafts ended up in the wastepaper basket.

From this experience I know that a deadline can be both

life and death to a piece of writing and that death is some-times preferable. It depresses me utterly to see children being forced to finish a piece of writing when they're sick of it, lacking in inspiration, and getting negative feedback in writing conferences. No one forces me to finish my writing, and I'm a published writer, so why should any writer be ruled in such a manner by someone who doesn't own the writing anyway?

Drafting and **conferencing** are the last two elements of this method I'd like to consider. It's the question of drafting and how it's approached that makes me want to scream and beat my head against a wall covered with graffiti attacking nonwriting teachers of writing. I can hardly find nice words to use to express my sorrow at the level of understanding of what drafting is. It is not, for me, any rigid set of rules. I don't write a rough draft, conference, reorder, conference, re-write, conference, and then write out my final draft. Every time I write, my need to draft is different. The idea of three drafts each time (which is current in some schools) is applying Graves's ideas in a way that must make him tear his hair out in despair. Only nonwriters could ask for three drafts. Why three? Why not two? Or thirty-two?

I never outline. In writing this chapter I drafted eleven different leads. I could not continue beyond my leads because the lead sets my tone and direction, and it's hard to write without those. I had to get the lead right. So far I haven't redrafted the whole chapter, but I have rewritten bits of it — many bits. I'm on page 7 of a writing pad, but I have twenty-six drafted pieces of paper scattered across the table. In a way this is still my first draft because I haven't written to this point in my argument until this moment. I need the drafts I need. So do kids. So do all writers.

When I'm angry I seem to be able to write with punch —

a first draft is all I need, and off goes the letter to the paper, the submission to the college administration, or the diatribe to the school about the wearing of uniforms. Some of my students, anxious to please, ask me what they can rewrite when both I and they love the first draft. We don't always have to draft. But how can we know that if we ourselves never write?

No one has conferenced me on this chapter. I didn't want it. I had talked and exploded about it to my family and friends so much before I started that I felt I couldn't burden them further. But that's unusual. I can be so bogged down that I will actually say to my husband, "Well, will you write the first paragraph then?" And I pass his work off as my own. Conferencing, like time and drafting, is an individual need that changes with every writing act. So of course I get mad when I hear a teacher, in a grim voice, say, "Now, Taylor, you haven't had a conference for a long time. What have you been up to?" It isn't the teacher's business to ask about a writer's conferencing needs, but how would we know that if we didn't use conferencing in different ways in our own struggle to write?

Donald Graves himself is concerned that his ideas have become an inflexible orthodoxy handed down from on high, on tablets of stone. They are wonderful ideas, flexible ideas, based in the real world of writers at work. They will fail only if we teachers of writing refuse to write ourselves, to learn firsthand the fear of rejection; the fear of self-exposure; the horror of writing; the pleasure of having an appreciative audience; and the necessity for a reason, a reader, and a real reaction. We ourselves must write in order to spread the word with conviction.

How do I, as a teacher, organize myself to write? I have a group of six friends, all of whom teach writing, who provide me with an audience at least one evening a month, over nibbles and coffee, or stronger. We share our pieces about home, work, life, children, colleagues, hopes, memories, and so on in an atmosphere of noncompetitive trust. If it weren't for the writing group, I would hardly write at all, because I need an audience so badly. The purpose is to entertain, persuade, inform, or just share. My deadline is usually met a couple of hours before we are due to meet — most of us write only in the twenty-four hours before our meeting. If we need the group to confer with us on an important article or submission, the group is happy to do it. We laugh over our wickedness in presenting first drafts most of the time. We grin over the fact that some pieces are unfinished because they were only begun a few hours previously. We give critical help seriously when it's asked for. What we all know is that we would never write, outside the requirements of our work, if we didn't have the group to write for. A writing group within school or outside it, or just one receptive friend, gives courage and purpose to any guilty nonwriter who wishes to reform.

Already the grave of this new methodology has been dug by conservatives on the attack. If we don't take care, the grave will shortly be filled in, and a lovely gravestone will mark it: "Here lie the remains of the best methods in writing ever known upon this earth, killed by the inaction of nonwriting teachers of writing. R.I.P."

We could put a stop to the funeral service if we ourselves picked up our pens and began, in real earnest, to write.

4 A Fox in Possum's Clothing

The Teacher Disguised as Writer in Hot Pursuit of Literacy

Like St. Paul, I too have seen the light. It happened at the National Language Arts Conference in Western Australia in 1979, which I attended as a lecturer in drama to talk about storytelling; what I learned about reading literally changed my life. I left the conference inspired, praying to be involved in the teaching of reading and writing. My prayers were answered, and so it came to pass that in 1981 I was not only allowed to retrain by the college I work for but was encouraged to do so. Unlike Lot's wife, I never looked back.

In this chapter I'll be attempting a number of things. First, I'd like to illustrate the effect that my knowledge of the reading process has had on the way I write for young children. Then I'll be exploring some other influences in my life and work that affect my writing and teach me about how children learn to read and write — influences we don't hear much about at language arts conferences because they're not scientific or rational and can't be academically pinned down.

We know that the child is father to the man or, in my case, mother to the woman. I was a fortunate child who grew up in a typical language-arts-ideal home. I'm the living product of the book-filled house, with parents who read and valued literature, parents whom I often observed at their own desks, writing, and parents who made time to share and listen to the things that we children were reading and writing.

I remember picture books from very early on, one in particular published in 1946, the year I was born. It was called *The Chicken Book*, by Garth Williams, and began as follows:

Said the first little chicken,
With a queer little squirm,
"I wish I could find
A fat little worm."
Said the next little chicken,
With an odd little shrug,
"I wish I could find
A fat little slug. . . ."

I was overjoyed to find that *The Chicken Book* had been reprinted. I fell upon it with cries of delight and could once again hear my parents' voices reading it aloud to me as a child. Books like that have been the foundation of my present life as a reader, writer, and teacher. So at this point I'd like to thank my parents for providing me with the beautiful books that were to become an antidote for the later horror of school basal readers.

I then became a mother and tried to create a literary past for my own child that was as rich as my own had been. I didn't begin very well. When Chloë was only eighteen months old, I tried to teach her to read with a set of huge red flash cards that I spread out all over the back lawn. With the un-suspecting child in my arms, I ran shrieking from flash card to flash card, yelling the words at the top of my voice as she laughed and laughed. What I recall most from that incident is not Chloë's being able to read flash cards (she soon forgot them all, anyway) but the marvelous, gutsy warmth of our relationship. It continued as we shouted our way through Dr. Seuss's *Marvin K. Mooney* and Maurice Sendak's *Where the Wild Things Are.* We didn't always shout her books, but that's the sort of exuberance I most remember. Through books she bonded with my husband and me, and through my husband and me she bonded with books. That's been very important to me as a writer, and I'll be returning to it later.

So in 1979, before my age of enlightenment, I knew about being a child and being a mother, but I didn't know about being a teacher of reading. Now I do. More recently, listen-ing to speakers such as Margaret Spencer and Frank Smith, I have discovered that I'm a sort of two-headed teacher of read-ing: I teach reading, as most of us do, using other people's texts; but I also teach reading by virtue of being a writer for young children.

When I heard Frank Smith claim that writers are the *only* people who really teach reading — and writing, too, for that matter — I realized I'd been too flippant about my role as a writer for young children and was jolted into taking myself seriously. Because learning to read can't be separated from learning to write, I'm aware that I do teach writing through the way that I write — as well as teaching reading. However, my brief for this chapter is reading, so that will be my focus.

What *do* I know about reading, and what difference does it make? By now I guess we all know about the three cueing systems that we use in order to make sense of print:

- Knowledge of the world (semantic).
- Knowledge of language (syntactic).
- Knowledge of print (graphophonic).

Along with that, I also know these things about how we learn to read:

- We know that we don't read individual words or letters — instead we read whole chunks of print at a glance.
- We know that reading for meaning is more important than reading every word accurately.
- We know that reading is about guessing what's to come based on prior knowledge of what has gone before — in the text we're reading, as well as in our life experiences.
- We know that beginning readers need easy, interesting texts with plenty of rhyme, rhythm, and repetition, which will enhance their ability to predict what is to come.
- And we know that stories are much easier to read than lists of random words because stories have a structure and a context that support the making of meaning.

However, I'm also a parent and a storyteller, and my hunch is that there's more to reading than any of these, as I hope to demonstrate.

There are occasions when I write purely as a writer — when I forget the reading process entirely because the content is so urgent that it overrules my academic understanding. I wrote a picture-book story called *Sophie* about birth, living, dying, and death, and I never once remembered or thought about the reading process during the writing of it. It's only fifteen lines long. Chloë, who was then a typical seventeen-year-old embarrassed by her mother's writing, cried for two hours over that story. So why should I worry about vocabulary and rhyme, rhythm, and repetition?

On other occasions it's exactly the opposite — I'm so aware of the reading process and of teaching reading that I almost lose sight of art. I've written two upmarket basal readers, *A Cat Called Kite* and *Zoo Looking*, for two different publishing houses, both of which are to be congratulated on producing "real books" in their reading schemes. But I don't think I'll write any more basal readers, even if they are "real books." It's a deadly hazard, that tightrope walk between overtly teaching because you want to and incidentally teaching because you've produced stunning literature. I walk the tightrope all the time, but I hope that if I ever fall off, it will be a spectacular spill onto the art side.

Let's explore the three cueing systems. The first is "knowledge of the world." I was aware of that when I wrote *Possum Magic*. I built on the familiar, such as Vegemite sandwiches, but I also felt a duty to extend the horizons of my readers by including all the state capitals of Australia and by making it clear that Tasmania was an island state: " 'You look wonderful, you precious possum!' said Grandma Poss. 'Next stop, Tasmania!' And over the sea they went." It was done deliberately. I was teaching reading by providing my readers information that would become prior knowledge in their subsequent reading of other texts.

The second cueing system is "knowledge of language." The children I write for are so young that they're still immersed in the rhyme and rhythm of nursery and playground rhymes. I wanted to build on that background, to connect that world to the world of books, so I included rhyme in *Possum Magic*, right there, in the middle of the prose: "She looked into this book and she looked into that. There was magic for thin and magic for fat, magic for tall and magic for small, but the magic she was looking for wasn't there at all."

In my local newspaper on August 20, 1983, the children's literature critic wrote, "If I dislike the way the story every now and then falls suddenly into rhyme and just as suddenly out again, that is a small and perhaps purely personal fault to find with what is almost perfection." But it's the rhyming that children love — and remember! When I went to a school in a poverty-stricken area of Adelaide to talk to some rough, tough, spunky sixth graders, a twelve-year-old girl saw *Possum Magic* under my arm. She didn't know I'd written it: "Ah, I love that book! 'Magic for thin and magic for fat, magic for tall and magic for small.' " The rhyming had been vindicated.

And now to the third of the cueing systems, "knowledge of print." I have never yet written a "Dan-can-fan-the-man" book, and of course I never will. I am aware, however, that some attention, somewhere along the line, has to be paid to graphophonics. In my second book, *Wilfrid Gordon McDonald Partridge*, I had a huge battle with the publishers — a battle I lost — over the names of the old people. I wanted "Mrs. Morgan, who played the organ"; "Mr. Lawry, who told scary stories"; "Mrs. Hicks, who walked with wooden sticks"; and "Mr. Bryant, who had a voice like a giant." I could see the teaching possibilities. I could see the learning possibilities. I was imbued with the fire of the knowledge of the reading process! To my chagrin we now have Mrs. Jordan playing the organ, Mr. Tippet being crazy about cricket, and so on. The publishers thought rhyming names were beyond the realm of reality. Publishers of children's fiction would do well to attend a language arts conference or two. They have much to learn.

I don't simplify vocabulary because I don't feel hidebound by the graphophonic cueing system. I know that meaning isn't difficult to grasp because we read in chunks, so I never worried about the apparently long words in *Possum Magic* such as *invisible, pavlova, lamington,* or *Vegemite sandwiches*. (A lamington is a delicious, typically Australian, chocolate-and-coconut sponge cake.) When I read *Possum Magic* to five-year-olds, I have to prepare the muscles in my face not to smile when I come to the sentence "In Hobart, late one night, they saw a lamington on a plate" because there's nearly always a heartfelt chorus of "Ah, yu-u-u-m!" It's the "Ah, yum!" that teaches the kids how to read, not the length of the word *lamington*.

Reading one book teaches us how to read another. It's one of the "prior knowledge" factors in reading. So, along with knowledge of the world, and language, and print, children need to develop a knowledge of how books work. That's why *Possum Magic* starts with "Once upon a time"; children have heard it before and will hear it again. That's why *Possum Magic* is an archetypal quest story; it prepares its readers for Victor Kelleher's *Master of the Grove,* Tolkien's *Lord of the Rings,* the Arthurian legends, and the *Odyssey* of Homer.

What else do I know about the reading process? I know that rhythm and repetition are important as aids to prediction, so I used them to extremes in *Guess What?* and *Hattie and the Fox. Hattie* connects to children's pasts through the story of the Little Red Hen, and Pat Hutchins's *Rosie's Walk,* and is a foundation for the future of Chaucer's Chaunticleer and Dame Partlett in "The Nun's Priest's Tale." I try to remember my place in the continuum of literature, acting as a carefully built bridge between past and future. Here's a bit of *Hattie* to show you what I mean:

Hattie was a big black hen.
One morning she looked up and said,

"Goodness gracious me! I can see a nose in the
  bushes!"
"Good grief!" said the goose.
"Well, well!" said the pig.
"Who cares?" said the sheep.
"So what?" said the horse.
"What next?" said the cow.
And Hattie said, "Goodness gracious me!
I can see a nose and two eyes in the bushes!"
"Good grief!" said the goose.
"Well, well!" said the pig.
"Who cares?" said the sheep.
"So what?" said the horse.
"What next?" said the cow.

Imagine how happy I was to find this cow, horse, and sheep
quote from Frank Smith (1983):

> If you know what a word is likely to be, it is not
> difficult to use phonics to confirm or reject a partic-
> ular expectation. . . . Children who can predict that
> the next word is likely to be either *cow, horse* or *sheep*
> will not need much knowledge of spelling to sound
> correspondences to decide which it is. In fact it is
> through such prediction that a mastery of *useful*
> phonics is acquired. (p. 31)

Something else that I know about reading — and have
mentioned before — is that we read in chunks and our prime
aim is to make meaning. I try, therefore, to write *meaningfully.* I have written an anti-nuclear-war allegory in picture-

book form called *Feathers and Fools*, the depth of whose meaning is reflected by my choice of words:

> One day, a peacock, musing on the mysteries of life, said, "How strange that swans should swim. It is fortunate indeed that we do not, for we should surely drown."
>
> The other peacocks pecked and strutted, contemplating the meaning of this profound observation.
>
> Again the first peacock spoke. "How strange that swans should fly. It is happy indeed that we do not, for we should surely look ridiculous."
>
> The other peacocks pecked and strutted again, contemplating the meaning of this second observation.
>
> Again the first peacock broke the silence. "I fear the swans," he said. "They have great strength. If they wished they could turn us out of our gardens, or make us fly, or force us to swim."
>
> Here and there, peacock feathers rustled uneasily.
>
> "Alas!" cried one. "No home! No happiness! No life!"
>
> There followed anxious mutterings and a making of plans.

I couldn't have written that story had I not read Hans Christian Andersen, the Bible, Rudyard Kipling, and John Keats's "La Belle Dame Sans Merci." I deliberately included an overtly literary vocabulary because I remembered Chloë at six relishing — and quickly being able to read — the extraordinarily exciting vocabulary in Tomi Ungerer's *The Beast of Monsieur Racine*, which includes such gems as the following:

> Upon closer examination, he discovered strange footprints the predator had left behind. Footprints of a weird nature, indeed. It looked as if the ground had been trampled by stumps rather than feet. "Outrageous, positively outrageous!" exclaimed the victim.

I think there's a lesson there. E. B. White, the author of *Charlotte's Web*, believes that

> anybody who writes down to children is simply wasting . . . time. You have to write up, not down. Children are demanding. . . . Children love words that give them a hard time, provided they are in a context that absorbs their attention.

I have now covered what I know about reading except to add that some books help children to learn to read, and some help them to want to read. I'm aware of writing both sorts of books. Sometimes, as in *Koala Lou* (my personal favorite), which has a strong emotional pull as well as a repeating catchphrase, I kill two birds with one stone so that my readers, I hope, will both learn to read and want to read because of it.

Language arts conferences do not, I feel, provide all the answers to questions about reading, just the academic ones, about the process itself — very useful indeed, but not the complete picture. I have hunches about reading from my observations as a parent and as a storyteller that have influenced the way I teach reading — disguised as a writer.

First, I'm a parent. I remember all that bonding between

Chloë and Malcolm and books and me. So I write *about* relationships. I'm sure a love of reading is closely connected to a
love of the feeling of being read to by someone you love. I
write for the child-within-the-parent who is reading to the
child. I'd like adults to remember the best bits of their childhood as they read my books. I always write with adult readers
in mind because my readers are often too young to read on
their own. That's why there's the adult joke about "pumpkin
scones in Brisbane" in *Possum Magic*. (The wife of a premier
of Queensland, whose capital is Brisbane, was famous for her
pumpkin scones.) That's why the mother is so warm, understanding, and middle-class controlled for most of the book
called *Just Like That*, until at the end she's yelling her head
off while the child stands there, just like that. I can hear in
that story the adult-reader and the child-listener building up
to a crescendo of a relationship as they read it. If I can help
along the bonding between parents and children through my
books, I have a hunch I'll be helping along the bonding between children and literature.

I think one of the main problems with basal readers is
that in general their texts don't excite the adult reader, let
alone the poor little learners, so there's no bonding between
anyone or anything, and it's all very sad. The question that
arises out of this hunch about bonding is, How do we get *love*
into classrooms and libraries? A great Ph.D. dissertation topic
would be "The Role of Love in the Mastery of Reading"; I
hope someone tackles it soon.

I've noticed something else in our family of readers that's
closely connected with all this love stuff: we share what we
read, either during or after. All of us read bits of *The Secret
Diary of Adrian Mole Aged 13¾* aloud to each other, even
though the others had already read it. Chloë once wrote a

highly diversionary tale inspired by *Adrian Mole*, and she shared
it, laughing at her own jokes even before she read them out.
It was painful, sometimes boring, and often hilarious. We are,
I notice, a little community of readers and writers. When I
first read *The Color Purple* by Alice Walker, I phoned three
friends who'd read it already and wept buckets as I talked
about it. I wanted to share it. When my husband read Shirley
Hazzard's *The Transit of Venus*, his jaw hit the floor as he
finished the last page. I'd already read the book. "My God!"
he said. "What about the plane crash!" One of the pleasures
of a good book is having people close by to share it with, to
pass it on to, to borrow it from. The question that arises is,
How do we get that haphazard, crazy, loving sharing into
classrooms and libraries? As a writer I'm fortunate – I know
that my books are shared because, as I've already said, my
readers are often too young to read alone.

I have some other hunches about reading. I know from
watching Chloë that it's the emotional content in the material
she reads that makes her go on reading and reading and reading. (Clearly the flash cards did her no lasting harm.) I remember the thrill of horror we both experienced over *Are
You My Mother?* by P. D. Eastman and *The Giant Devil Dingo*
by Dick Roughsey when she was three. Then it was the laughs
she looked for – she read everything written by Tom Sharpe;
adored *The Hitchhiker's Guide to the Galaxy*, by Douglas Adams;
and knew *Adrian Mole* by heart. Conversely, when she read
Robert Cormier's *I Am the Cheese* for the first time, she was
so appalled that she sat in silence on the front veranda, staring
into space.

"What's the matter?" I said.

"That book! That book!"

So I try not to write pap. I think of Chloë and her books,

and I try to write *guts* instead. That's why I wrote in *Possum Magic*, "Grandma Poss looked miserable. 'Don't worry,' said Hush. 'I don't mind.' But in her heart of hearts she did." The problem is there, admitted, but later resolved. The question that arises is, Where is the emotional content in most basal readers? The conflict? The fear? The heartache? The humor?

While conflict, fear, heartache, and humor may be desirable, they are not, by themselves, sufficient to hold the attention of readers or listeners. I've discovered that, through storytelling. The plot may be filled with blood and guts, but it's fine writing that keeps the audience rapt: it's exquisitely constructed sentences; it's carefully honed cadences; it's the marvelous satisfaction of the sensual rhythm of perfect prose.

As the child of missionaries, I am not unfamiliar with the sentence rhythms of the Bible. In fact, I'm sure I owe my love of literature, and my avid interest and excitement in the rhythms of writing, to my early exposure to the Bible and to my later exposure — at drama school — to the speaking of Shakespeare.

The storyteller-in-me insists that the writer-in-me writes well. I know the importance of beginnings and endings, so I try to hear an anonymous reader reading my words aloud: "Once upon a time but not very long ago, deep in the heart of the Australian bush lived two possums. Their names were Hush and Grandma Poss." I rewrote that first paragraph twenty-three times and literally cried with frustration in my attempt to get it right. To love a story, for me, means also to love its ending. Endings are crucial, so again I hear the parent's read-aloud voice saying, "From that time onwards Hush was visible. But once a year, on her birthday, she and Grandma Poss ate a Vegemite sandwich, a piece of pavlova, and half a lamington, just to make sure that Hush stayed visible forever. And she did."

In the light of all this, I do believe that the language of basal readers isn't good enough. Where are *their* magic beginnings and gentle endings? Even those of us involved in writing the real-book readers for enlightened publishers would do well to remember the poetic language of the Bible as we "write to teach." *Fine writing teaches reading whether we intend it to or not.* Fine writing ought to be our top priority.

And finally, I'd like to focus on the role of illustrations in the development of literacy. As a writer of picture books, where would I be without the pictures? It isn't only I who would be lost but also all the young readers for whom my books are springboards to literacy. The appeal of books, I've noticed, from Chloë, myself, my husband, and the many others I've observed, is not just in the rhyme, rhythm, and repetition, or in the plot, or in the emotional content, or even in the fine writing — it's in the pictures. Books that delight the eye first may later delight the ear, the heart, and the mind — but it is the *eye* first. So, while we're all busily writing in order to teach reading, I believe we're wasting our time utterly if the integrity of our texts is not matched by a similar integrity in the artwork. I can begin to understand the flamboyant bestselling success of *Possum Magic* when I see children actually stroking the pages because the fur looks so real. The entire book — its feel, its look, its smell, and its story — is a combination, designed to delight as a *whole.* It's through that delight that I see children both learning to read and wanting to read, and I am deeply thankful to Julie Vivas for her genius in creating the visual magic of our book.

Whereas, alas and alack, let's take a look at one of my upmarket "readers," *Zoo Looking.* The aim of this series is to produce readers disguised as "real books." It is a worthy aim, which I fully support. Real books delight. Basal readers don't.

But in *Zoo Looking* the illustrations and design are so down-market that the disguise has slipped and few kids will be tricked into imagining that it's a real book. Top-quality illustrations not only sell books to children, parents, teachers, and librarians but also sell *reading* to children, so we ignore them at our peril.

Hattie and the Fox was published by a different branch of the publisher that produced *Zoo Looking*, but what a world of difference there is between the two books. I wrote *Hattie* with the reading process firmly fixed in my mind. It could easily have been a banal basal reader, but Patricia Mullins's artwork has raised it to a delicious level. It's a real book; it's not pretending to be one.

As I rush headlong down the road toward children's literacy, heavily disguised as a beautifully painted possum, I have these thoughts in my fox's head: First, I like children. I like them very much. I have enormous respect for their intelligence and ability, and high hopes for their future. I haven't mentioned that before, but it is pivotal to my writing. Second, I'm happy that within the me who writes for children there is also a child, a parent, a teacher, and a storyteller because each of these provides me with different information and a unique perspective. The total picture I have as a writer leads me to conclude that loving relationships, fine writing, and stunning illustrations make learning to read an easy pleasure.

5 | Lessons from a Home

Homes, as I have already pointed out, have much to teach us about teaching and about the development of literacy. Long before they enter school, children achieve a number of significant skills at home, none of which is specifically taught. They learn how to sit up, how to walk and talk, how to dress themselves, and how to eat politely — more or less!

They acquire these skills because they need these skills. They acquire these skills because they have observed these skills in others: they observe how much faster and more efficient it is to walk than it is to crawl, so they learn to walk. They acquire these skills without a teacher coming into the home for daily instruction.

Clearly the family and the home environment are doing something right in terms of teaching. What is this something? What can we as teachers of literacy learn from parents? Sixteen tentative answers follow.

Lesson One:
Beware the Me/Them Separation Syndrome

Parents do not role-play teachers. They don't separate themselves from their children: they live with them daily in an atmosphere filled with affection and respect. When their children happen to learn a new skill they — the parents — do not stand back, aloof, handing out grades. Instead they show great delight and warm encouragement. There is no artificial distance between parent and child, yet the child is able to learn.

I remember watching a three-year-old boy "read" a fairly complex picture book to his grandmother and marveling at the shared laughter, the relaxed warmth of their togetherness, and the brilliance of the child. "He's not really brilliant," admitted the father. "It's just that he loves his grandma so much he'll do anything to be with her. Shared reading provides that opportunity. They read together all the time."

The boy and his grandmother were not distanced from each other emotionally in the way teachers and pupils are often distanced, and the learning was not separated from their mutual delight. I have attempted to remember this learning-through-delight in order to bring its power into my formal teaching situations. I don't always remember how important good relationships are.

Lesson Two:
Aim for the Stars, Not the Mud

Parents expect their children to talk, so they talk. Yet we don't expect our children to read before school — foolishly! Our own

Chloë was, to our amazement, "reading" by the age of two and a half: words such as *Exit, Stop,* BP, *Shell, Woolworth's,* and *Turn Left Any Time with Care.* Neither my husband nor I set out to teach her these signs, but she learned them anyway because we yelled them out for fun to keep her interested on car journeys. We did not aim to teach — we aimed to have fun. In fact, had we been told at her birth that she would be "reading" at the age of two we wouldn't have believed it. What child, we would have scoffed, could learn to read at the age of two? In terms of Chloë's literacy our expectations were at the mud level, not way up among the stars.

It is worth restating one of the essences in the previous chapter: that we did, however, read books to Chloë, loving the child-parent togetherness as much as we loved the stories. Eventually we read books *with* her. And then, at four and a half, she read all by herself. We were astonished and thrilled. As a teacher myself I learned two lessons from my child's development of literacy: First, we expect too little of the children in our care, be they in our homes or in our classrooms. Second, when books are read for their intended purposes of entertaining and informing, and when that entertainment and information bonds readers and listeners in mutual delight, learning to read becomes an almost natural activity and an enormous pleasure.

Lesson Three:
Beware of Teachers' College Knowledge

At teachers' college most of us learn about something called child development; we receive the information that a child of such and such an age will be able to do this and that, not much more, and not much less. This tends to fix our expectations of children's capabilities. We don't expect a four-year-old boy to write a book and illustrate it. A four-year-old? Write a book? How could such a phenomenon be possible? Our expectations carry us along in a lowest-common-denominator groove — a groove we find hard to climb out of. We are blinkered by the narrow vision permitted us in child development courses. Consequently we gasp when we are presented, as I was, with a three-page "book" written and illustrated without any adult assistance by Carl Nilsson-Polias, aged four:

> Was apon a tam
> a boy wan to the shops
> an cam hom ign

The lesson Carl taught me was never to be surprised by the literacy children attained by any particular age but to expect the highest achievement always and always to reward it with enormous delight.

Lesson Four:
Is Your Hair Carefully Coiffured?

Glenn Domann, the creator of the famous "Teach Your Baby to Read" kit, discovered in his research that the mothers of educationally subnormal children who were the most successful in helping their children to read were those who fell into the "dizzy blonde" category. However, not all were blonde! What these women had in common was an abundance of energetic excitement, which spilled out whenever their children achieved another skill, learned a new word, or read another sentence. Their joy was manifestly obvious to their offspring, who in turn felt so happy in their mothers' happiness that they tried hard to elicit that happiness and excitement again and again, thereby improving their literacy skills in leaps and bounds. The "tight" mothers with restrained personalities, impeccable clothes, and perfect manners were less able to "hang loose" and celebrate their children's achievements at the appropriate moments. Their tightness led to less satisfactory improvements in their children's reading ability.

From this I learned, as a teacher, to be a little crazy in the classroom, to let no improvement go unnoticed, and to be noisy in my praise and lavish in my joy. It's made my teaching exhausting but a lot of fun: there's so much, I've discovered, to be excited about.

Lesson Five:
Beware the Yawn!

When Chloë was young I read to her every night, and most of the books I read I loved. If I read a book, by chance, that I did not enjoy, I never read it to her again. I was frightened that my nonenjoyment of reading a particular book would put her off reading. I believed that my enthusiasm for a story would sell her that great attraction called reading, just as much as the story itself. Enthusiasm has much to be said for it in the development of literacy, which is why I would never read a basal reader to Chloë, to myself, or to any group of children in my educational care. And if I had my way, *no* child learning to read would ever be exposed to the bound-to-be-boring banality of basal readers. I yawn over basals. So do children.

The yawn is a danger signal. We would do well to remember it and to avoid it.

Lesson Six:
Burn the Blasted Basals!

This lesson follows directly from lesson five: A school principal who, like me, yawned over basals decided once and for all to be rid of them. She considered them to be pollution, to be filth, to be detrimental to children's advancement toward literacy, so — unbeknownst to her startled staff — she burned all the basals in her school, pile by pile, in the school incinerator one summer holiday. At the beginning of the new school year, amid the wails and panic of her teachers, she set in motion a whole-language program in which real books were used in the classroom, including books the children wrote themselves. I believe some of her teachers never forgave her for her extreme action, but the children certainly did — not only were they able to learn to read more easily but they also *wanted* to read. In this school "wanting to read" had previously been a rare phenomenon. A revolution had occurred.

Lesson Seven:
Be Seen to Sob over Sob Stories

Children usually want to engage in activities they observe their parents enjoying. Because, on the whole, parents read after their children are in bed, not many children see their parents engrossed in a book. We might do well to redress this situation. If children don't know we love to read, how will they realize what an absorbing, rewarding activity reading is?

I recall sobbing in a foreign airport over the ending of *Villette*, by Charlotte Brontë. My husband was sitting a few meters away engrossed in a newspaper. "Sob, sob, sob," I cried. "Sob, sob, sob." Chloë, then aged thirteen, hissed into my ear, "Ma, if you don't pull yourself together people will think you and Pop are getting divorced." At least she could see that reading a book provided me with something important enough to howl over. I remember years later beginning to read A. S. Byatt's *Possession* at about 3:00 P.M. one Saturday and not being able to move from the couch until well after our usual evening mealtime. The book, it was clear, had transcended my family's nutritional needs. I pretended the family didn't exist. The Power of the Book had been exposed, and an important lesson had been revealed: that reading can be a totally absorbing and intensely rewarding activity.

Those two occasions, in which I accidentally demonstrated a love of reading, made me think that we need, as teachers, to be seen reading and loving to read *in class*, in front of the children. We need to be seen laughing over books, being unable to put books down, sobbing over sob stories, gasping over horror stories, and sighing over love stories — anything, in fact, that helps our students to realize that there is some reward, that there are *many* rewards, to be had from the act of reading.

Lesson Eight:
Stop Teaching Reading and Start Teaching Readers

Although I learned to read using basal readers, their boring content did not teach me that I could be a lifelong reader. Children exposed only to basals may indeed learn to read, but they find the stories so lifeless and so tedious that they wonder why people *bother* to read: they don't become lifelong readers because no one has ever given them a reason to be lifelong readers. We need real books in the classroom, books beautifully written and beautifully produced, wild books, funny books, scary books, sad books, loving books, short books, long books, picture books, chapter books, nonfiction books — anything that will create *rewarded* readers.

I think six-year-old Deng, in the following letter to me, might be pleading for the opportunity to read real books in his classroom. It's obvious from the last line that Rachel, who was my student and Deng's student teacher, had read aloud my book *Koala Lou*, which contains this recurring line: "Koala Lou, I DO love you!"

*to mem fox i huldle red books so I huldle notes yoru books
nsemt in klus wen Rachel reds books of yoru and nele
evre book that she res is wan of yoru books and naw I
sink I like to red yoru books ynow and I wis thay put
sam of yoru book into some books like books that I red
from scöll I dont now*

> *But do you I do love you*
> *Deng*

[*To Mem Fox I hardly read books so I hardly notice your books except in class when Rachel reads books of yours and nearly every book that she reads is one of your books and now I think I like to read your books you know and I wish they put some of your books into some books like books that I read from school I don't know But do you I do love you Deng.*]

Lesson Nine:
Forget the Singing Nun

In *The Sound of Music* the nun Maria sings the following: "When you read you begin with ABC, When you sing you begin with do re mi. . . ." She's wrong. When you read you don't begin with ABC because individual letters are difficult to recognize on their own, without any supporting context. It's easier, much easier to recognize words such as apple, ball, and cat than it is to recognize *A*, *B*, or *C*. In fact, the more support there is around letters and words, the easier reading becomes because there's so much else in the text that points the reader in the right direction for meaning making. So it is actually easier to read a story than it is to read a paragraph, easier to read a paragraph than a sentence, easier to read a sentence than a word, and easier to read a word than to recognize a letter.

The lesson to be learned from this information is to begin the teaching of reading by reading with whole stories aloud, using Big Books whenever it's appropriate or possible. This will create readers as well as teach reading.

Lesson Ten:
Kill the Idea that Kids Can't

If we allowed children to show us what they *can* do rather than merely accepting what they usually do, I feel certain we would be in for some grand surprises. As adults our feeble expectation of children's capabilities puts brakes on their potential.

I did not expect Chloë, aged nine, to be able to read and enjoy Jane Austen's *Pride and Prejudice*. She had watched three episodes of it on television before she asked if we had a copy of it in the house because she wanted to know how the story ended. Did Darcy marry Elizabeth? That was the crucial question. It was on the tip of my tongue to say, "Yes, and we do have *Pride and Prejudice* in the house, but you're much too young to read it." I stopped myself just in time. She wanted to read it, she needed to read it, so she did read it. I was astounded. *If we allowed children to show us what they could do* they would probably learn a lot faster than we permit them to, at present.

Lesson Eleven:
Eliminate the Idiotic Interfering Adult

As adults we choose our own reading material. Depending on our moods and needs we might read the newspaper, a block-buster novel, an academic article, a women's magazine, a comic, a children's book, or the latest book that just about *everyone* is reading. No one chastises us for our choice. No one says, "That's too short for you to read." No one says, "That's too easy for you, put it back." No one says, "You couldn't read that if you tried — it's much too difficult."

Yet if we take a peek into classrooms, libraries, and book-shops we will notice that children's choices are often mocked, censured, censored, and denied as valid by idiotic, interfering teachers, librarians, and parents. Choice is a personal matter that changes with experience, changes with mood, and changes with need. We should let it be.

Someone had told a sixteen-year-old illiterate that Nathaniel Hawthorne's book *The Scarlet Letter* was about a prostitute. He wanted to read it. He was determined to read it. "If that book's about a whore I'm gonna read it!" he declared. And he did, even though the language is nineteenth-century English and much of the vocabulary unfamiliar. It took him a long time, but he learned to read because no one laughed at him when he said, "I'm gonna read it." Let's stop laughing at kids. Let's leave our mocking voices outside. Let's stop being idiotic, interfering adults who won't allow children the same freedom of choice we accord to ourselves.

Lesson Twelve:
Water the Desert and Watch It Bloom

A common cry from children-as-writers is this: "I don't know what to write about." Topics and ideas are hard to find, it's true, but they're harder to find if children are living in a literary desert. Basal readers provide no ideas: no humor, no exquisite story structure, no consequences, no real heroes or heroines, no heavenly language that repeats or rhymes or beats its way through a story, no emotions at all. This literary desert is an ideas desert when it comes to knowing what to write about.

We need to water the desert so that the writing will bloom. By *watering the desert* I mean providing children with the most wonderful literature available: the classics, the new, the beautiful, the revolting, the hysterical, the puzzling, the amazing, the riveting. We need to fill their storehouses with events, characters, styles, emotions, places, and themes that will help them to grow, not wither, thirsty in the desert of illiteracy.

Lesson Thirteen:
Read Aloud, Alive, a Lot

From my own experience I realize that the literature I *heard*, rather than read, as a child resonates again and again in my memory whenever I sit down to write. It's the sounds I remember rather than the sight of words. Of course silent reading also fills our storehouses, but it is an immediate treat to be read aloud to, especially when the reader reads in a lively manner, enthusiastically, using his or her voice expressively to paint vivid pictures in our imaginations.

Powerful writers and powerful speakers have two wells they can draw on for that power: one is the well of rhythm; the other is the well of vocabulary. But vocabulary and a sense of rhythm are almost impossible to "teach" in the narrow sense of the word. So how are children expected to develop a sense of rhythm or a wide vocabulary? By being read to, alive, a lot!

Lesson Fourteen:
Worksheets Make Wonderful Paper Planes

If the language we use in the classroom is not the same as the language we use in real life, surely we are wasting valuable time. When in real life do we ever write for no reason? For no response? When in real life do we write nonsense, in simple words, in sentences that have no consequence? Never! Yet in school we give children worksheets, ditto sheets, workbooks, and other similar nonsense.

Worksheets are the dead-end streets of literacy: there's a non-message on each line, going nowhere, for no reason, and without any hope of a message making a return journey of response back to the writer. Worksheets do not develop writers who can think for themselves, who can create extended texts, who can be logical, who can use voice or tone, or who can write with power. It is perfectly possible to be able to fill in endless worksheets correctly yet not be able to write a single coherent paragraph, let alone a longer piece of connected prose.

If we want to maintain *illiteracy*, worksheets are perfect. Actually I prefer making worksheets into paper planes — they fly through the air wonderfully. Paper planes don't stop kids from developing proficiency as writers. Paper planes are harmless. Worksheets are not.

Lesson Fifteen:
Bring in the Bathtub

A child was once heard to say, "I hate reading. My legs get tired." Clearly the only time the poor little thing read a book was to the teacher, standing beside teacher's desk. As far as I know most adults don't read standing up, by choice. On crowded trains it is sometimes necessary to read standing up, but most of us prefer to sit down, curl up, or lie down to read. Most of us don't read for pleasure, by choice, sitting upright at the kitchen table. Yet in school we expect children to read in physical situations of the utmost discomfort.

A first-grade teacher of my acquaintance, anxious to provide a more inviting physical environment for reading, brought an old bathtub into her classroom. It was battered and chipped but still steady on its old-fashioned claw feet. Into it the teacher tossed some pillows and soft cushions. How the kids loved to read in that bathtub! They settled in, three and four at a time, happy in their own books, away with their stories, in another world.

A bathtub is not the easiest answer for a friendly reading environment, but it may be a useful metaphor to keep in mind for the prevention of tired legs, stiff backs, and reluctant readers.

Lesson Sixteen:
Once More, with Feeling

Reading aloud is not a cure-all. Not quite. But it is such a wonderful antidote for turning on turned-off readers and brightening up dull writing that I feel it's worthwhile to plead again for its regular occurrence in every classroom, not only those classrooms at the younger end of the school. Even in my forties I have benefited as a writer *directly* from hearing writing read aloud. The music, the word choice, the feelings, the flow of the structure, the new ideas, the fresh thoughts — all these and more are banked in my writing checking account whenever I am fortunate enough to be read to. The value of my writing increases before my very eye, beneath my very pen. The investment in *listening*, I have found, pays dividends.

That is why I'm closing these particular remarks in an attitude of supplication, begging for teachers to read aloud, once more, with feeling, every day of their classroom lives.

6 "Halt! Who Goes There?"

A Dialogue about Language Arts

The setting is a gathering of language arts teachers. The two main characters are the Language Arts Teacher and the Keeper At The Gate. Carrying a briefcase, the Language Arts Teacher moves toward the podium with the clear intention of making a statement, but she is stopped by the Keeper At The Gate.

KEEPER AT THE GATE: Halt! Who goes there?

LANGUAGE ARTS TEACHER: A teacher of language arts.

KATG: State your name.

LAT: Fox, Mem.

KATG: State your purpose.

LAT: I've come to speak to the Language Arts Thinkers.

KATG: I am the Keeper At The Gate. You may not pass.

LAT: But I must. It's urgent. Why may I not pass?

KATG: There are conditions that must be fulfilled.

LAT: Conditions? What conditions?

KATG: You must allow me to search your baggage for certain essentials. And for forbidden items.

LAT: Forbidden items? Such as comprehension exercises? A list of topics for children's writing? A red pen? A basal reading scheme? Please, *please*. Of course I haven't got those in my baggage. Didn't you hear what I said? I said I wanted to join the Language Arts Thinkers, not the Guardians of the Past Imperfect.

KATG: Rudeness will get you nowhere. Besides, you are being simplistic. I had already assumed that the items you mentioned would not be in your baggage. The forbidden items, I should warn you, are cheap remarks about those who might have different theories from your own. I won't be searching for anything so insignificant as *items*. I'll be looking instead for those things that take up most of the space in the baggage of language arts teachers: beliefs, understandings, theories, and practices. I'll be searching for proof that you are an original thinker, not a sheeplike follower of trends. And I shall want to find compelling supporting evidence behind any grand assertions you might make.

LAT: And if these things are not in my baggage, what then?

KATG: Why then you may join one of our other organizations: the Guardians of the Past Imperfect — whom you have already mocked — or the Bandwagon Riders.

LAT: Oh no, not the Bandwagon Riders! I joined them once, but not for long. There was just too much jumping on and off in the Bandwagon Riders. Besides, I used to get confused about which wagon I was supposed to be on at any given time, and I used to blush terribly if I found I was on the wrong one.

KATG: I understand. Open your bag. You may show me the contents in any order that you wish.

The Language Arts Teacher opens her briefcase and retrieves a sign saying "Relationships," which she shows to the KATG.

KATG: "Relationships." I see.

LAT: A parent, Alison, and an eighteen-month-old child, Tamara, are reading a book together. These are some of the elements of their relationship: Alison knows Tamara and loves her; she wishes the best for her child and will protect her from all possible evil and fright; she expects her to succeed to the best of her ability. Alison accepts that it is her responsibility to care for and nurture this child so that Tamara will reach her potential as a learner, a citizen, and an emotionally stable, happy human being. Alison is delighted to be in Tamara's company.

Tamara knows her mother and loves her; they get along so well together that Tamara behaves as nicely as she can:

she'd hate to spoil the relationship by disappointing her mother. She understands her mother's moods and knows how far she can go. She feels safe with her mother, knowing that she'll be protected from all possible evil and fright. She has physical, emotional, and intellectual needs, which she knows her mother will supply. The two of them share a past, the rituals of home life, outings, and family jokes. There is a sweetness of spirit between them. They are utterly comfortable together, and Tamara is learning new words and phrases rapidly and happily every day. She's learning so quickly she'll soon be able to speak as well as Alison does.

That's a true story, but it's seventeen years old. Alison is my sister, Tamara my niece. When Tam was five my sister had an accident in which she became a paraplegic, so Tam was not, after all, protected from all possible evil and fright. It had a terrible impact on her ability to learn in her first year at school.

When I teach language arts, I keep in mind the teaching/learning relationship between my sister and her child. First, they know each other, so I try to get to know my students as quickly as I can: their names, their pasts, their social situations, what they do in their spare time, their successes, their fears, and their wishes.

Second, my classroom is not my home, but remembering my sister and her child, I try to make it as emotionally informal and homelike as possible so that my students and I are, most of the time, delighted to be in each other's company. By chatting to them and writing them personal letters I discover a great deal about who they are. I also reveal a lot of myself in order to make it easier for them to get to know me and to understand who I am.

I reveal, for instance, that I am red-eyed and puffy-faced in class because I've been reduced to tears of rage by the politics in my university. I allow myself literally to leap around the classroom when one of my manuscripts has been accepted for publication so that the excitement isn't just mine, it's ours. I share the laughter and the horror of living with a twenty-one-year-old who once left home forever and then had the nerve to return four months later. If I have to leave my students to go to a conference, I tell them the gossip when I get back, such as how I met Donald Graves, Ken and Yetta Goodman, and Bill Martin Jr, or the story from the Las Vegas IRA conference in May 1991 when I was out visiting a school and asked the children to guess where I came from:

"California?"

"No."

"New York?"

"No."

"South America?"

"No. I'll give you a clue. It's a place where they have lots of koalas and kangaroos."

"The zoo?"

Third, remembering my sister and her child, I try to set an atmosphere of safety in which my students feel protected from all possible evil and fright so that they're relaxed and happy enough to learn. And, remembering how important my sister and child are to each other, I try to become as important a person to my students as they are to me so that *how I feel* really matters to them — I want them to care about doing their best so as not to disappoint me, let alone themselves. I am unashamedly present in my classroom as a pseudo parent of my vast student family because of the evidence of the effectiveness of families in allowing children to learn.

As in all families we have in-jokes. In one of my classes every student's assignment had its pages clipped together with a green paper clip. They all know that I love green paper clips, that I pry them off student papers whenever I can. I mention to my students that the only bribery I understand or accept is that of the green paper clip. So at the end of the semester when I beheld the beneficence of green paper clips, my heart skipped a beat. I was ecstatic — and not only on account of the paper clips. Clearly I had a terrific in-joke relationship with that class, so I wasn't surprised to discover that the level of work done by those students was consistently higher than that of any other class. As was the case with Alison and Tamara, these students and I liked each other very much indeed. We liked each other to the extent that it made a qualitative difference to my teaching and therefore also to their learning. There was a sweetness of spirit between us.

Stuart was one of these students. His final piece of writing had had the whole class shrieking with laughter. He'd written so cleverly and wittily about the stiffness and anxiety caused by his first day as a sheepshearer that it had been possible to believe, all the way through the piece, that he'd been writing about masturbating, of all things. We had been thrown off the scent partly by his northern English accent, which had seemed highly unlikely in a shearer.

The family understandings in our group and the comic tone and tastefulness of Stuart's writing made the topic perfectly acceptable. My jawbone ached from laughing. Like Tamara with Alison, Stuart knew how far he could go with me. In my audiotaped response to his piece I told him he was in the wrong profession — that he should be a stand-up comedian, not a teacher. I had meant it as a compliment, but as it turned out he misunderstood me.

He was naturally very upset to discover at the end of the semester that he was one of the students who had to write the final exam — an exam set for those naughty writers whose spelling, sentence structure, and punctuation have not reached my required high standards. One of the exam questions requested that the students write me a letter about what they'd change if they could change any one of the following: their parents, grandparents, or siblings; their car; the place they lived in; their partner; any of their college courses; their career; or their lives. For once I had set a topic to help them make a rapid choice, given the time constraints. Stuart wrote:

Dear Mem,

I really don't know what to write about. I suppose I would like to change my mother and father. But then again I wouldn't want to. I know, I'd like to change my life. Don't get me wrong, I'm loving university and I really want to be a teacher which is the reason why I got so upset when you told me to leave teaching to other people. What exactly did you mean by this? Do you think my accent is too hard to understand or was it because of all my mistakes? Please remember I was sick at the time.

I do worry about my mistakes all the time. If I could change my life this is what I would change. I'd be a more studious person and make sure that the mistakes I made would not be made again. I would make sure that the teachers I've had in the past would teach their students properly. I would change my past attitudes and be more reliable. There is nothing I would change about my present except being able to think of more to write about. But it was you who said . . . that a person can't be expected to write on command . . . I am having trouble writing on command. I also apologize for the fact that this letter is so short.

Your student,
Stuart

Stuart managed to turn the exam into an authentic piece of writing that had significance for him. He was able to reveal distress, confusion, and irritation. He proved he'd learned something about the difficulty of writing on command on a specific topic. And because he and I had, in the simplest terms, loved each other, he was able to punish me for hurting him by withholding his love at the end of the letter, which he had signed coldly: "Your student, Stuart." In earlier letters it had been "Love, Stuart." That he *had* affection he could withhold delighted me because it showed we belonged to the same tribe, as it were — the same family.

The setting for these events was not an elementary school — it was and is a university from which students drop out at an alarming rate because so often the relationships between teacher and taught are impersonal, forbidding, and discouraging — and in which neither teacher nor taught know each other's first names, or even each other's last names sometimes, let alone any humanizing personal information about one another.

I see no age difference in the fundamental need for good relationships in teaching/learning situations; I believe they arise from knowing those whom we teach and knowing those who teach us: from being open about our own lives and our own outside-school realities, and from caring about and knowing the different people in our classes. Good relationships are an essential part of my baggage, and I would have been devastated if I'd found that I had left them at home.

KATG: Why did you mention that your sister was paraplegic? Has this any relevance to the teaching of language arts?

LAT: Please don't ask me to be language-arts-specific just yet. I want to move from the global inward. I told you about my sister because I wanted to practice what I was preaching since this is, in effect, a teaching/learning situation. I wanted to establish a relationship with you by revealing something about my own family. I wanted to become, in your eyes, a human being who has been touched by tragedy rather than a cold figure pontificating from a podium. I felt that if you knew me you might begin to like me, and if you liked me you might listen more carefully and willingly to what I had to say.

KATG: I see. What else do you have in your baggage?

The Language Arts Teacher opens her suitcase and retrieves a sign saying "Reality," which she shows to the KATG.

KATG: "Reality." I see.

LAT: In a college staffroom a balding man is tearing out what remains of his hair, and as he does so he is groaning about student incompetence. "We asked them to write a letter to a principal," he says, "in which they set out their statement of beliefs in the hope of gaining employment in a middle school. They couldn't do it. They were absolutely hopeless! And that's when they were writing for a *purpose*, for heaven's sake!" I ask gently if the principal is actually real, if the students might expect a real reply, if there might be any real consequence arising from the writing of the letter other than that of passing or failing the course.

It transpires, as I feared, that the whole thing is a charade, not a reality. If a piece of writing doesn't really matter, then of course it doesn't really matter how it's written. The purpose of genuine literacy is to present a significant meaning to real people in the expectation of a personally significant reaction. What the balding academic has not understood is the lack of personal significance in the task he has set. No wonder it hasn't worked.

I once asked my students to tell me about the pieces of writing they'd done at school that stood out in their memory as particularly enjoyable or significant. Most of them couldn't. Of the few memorable pieces the most common was the children's book some of them had written in sixth grade to read to the second grade. At the time I had 150 students with twelve years each of schooling, forty-two weeks of the year, five days per week, and let's say a conservative two writing tasks a day — a total of 756,000 pieces of writing, and most of it forgettable! It's an outrageous statistic, especially if you believe, as I do, that writers rarely agonize over genre, content, tone, structure, clarity, and correctness unless their writing has real personal significance: that is, *when the consequences of having written actually matter to the writer.*

Phil Cummings, the Australian author of *Goodness Gracious!* and other books for children, put these consequences to me succinctly in a letter when he said, "Hell, I was wetting myself the day *Goodness Gracious!* was launched!" I ask myself how often our students get to a stage when they positively "wet themselves" over a piece of writing they've done in school. Sometimes? Rarely? Or never?

In Sean's case, rarely. Sean was a first-year student in 1990. In response to one of my articles (chapter 1 of this volume) he wrote:

> *Dear Mem,*
> *   Your article entitled "Notes from the Battlefield"*
> *turned out to be an interesting read. Realistically it didn't*

*make me launch into back flips across the back yard
but it did make me stop and think about why people
write . . . Looking back on my twelve years of schooling
I can recall only one or two instances where I wrote for a
purpose that was real to me rather than writing for a
mark. In both cases I was desperate for a positive response.*

*In Grade Seven I made the state team for football. I
went away to Sydney, played well and had a good time.
The trouble was, in doing so my mates didn't want to
know me — I was branded "The Big-Head." The following month of my life was living hell. Anyhow, on my return the principal made us write a one-page summary of
the trip which was to be printed in the weekly newsletter.
This meant every single student had to take one home,
read it and get their parents to sign it.*

*What was I to write? The truth? If I did that my
friends would never speak to me again. If I wrote lies or
seemed negative my mother would have killed me. She
had paid the $300 for me to go away. I sweated for
many nights over that bit of work. Even now, seven
years on I still regard that as being my most critical piece
of work.*

*Just in case you're interested I wrote about having a
good time but I clearly stated how I sat on the bench most
games and that even when I did play I got dragged off.
The end result pleased my parents and my peers.*

*It's funny because even when I write today it's like
I'm writing to that same group of people. I don't quite
say everything I want to say. Or if I do I'll re-word it so
it doesn't come across as being too strong.*

Sean's letter made me — and my colleagues — think hard
about the sorts of writing our own students have to do. We

decided we didn't want them to write assignments merely to pass our course. We wanted them to engage wholeheartedly (i.e., *affectively*) in their college writing tasks: to experiment, to be bold, to have fun, and yet to adhere to appropriateness in terms of genre, content, correctness, and so on. We, both staff and students, developed a test we could run on any writing task to analyze its significance and authenticity. We called it the Three W Test: Why? Who for? Who cares?

We reasoned that if writers don't know why they're writing, if they don't know whom they're writing for, and if the response to their writing is going to be so unimportant that they couldn't care less about it, they'll put in a minimum of effort; and we reasoned that the corollary of a minimum of effort would be a minimum of development.

Our students took off! Even the smallest and most mundane tasks, such as peer assessment of tutorials, became a worthwhile challenge.

Language Arts Evaluation

Which statement best describes our tutorial?
a. it was so exciting you wish you were us
b. so good you'd come again and bring your friends
c. pretty boring but it was better than a maths lecture
d. you felt like you didn't need a Ronald and Scott tutorial at 9–10 on a Tuesday morning
e. none of the above

Did you experience any joy from our tutorial?
a. no, we were bored shitless
b. it was OK, but . . .
c. it was mildly joyful
d. I was damn excited about it
e. it was near orgasmic

Apart from the (a) fun or (b) boredom did you on the off-chance actually learn anything and find it relevant? If yes, what? No? It doesn't matter then!

If you answered (a) in the previous question, would you use it in the classroom? And would you change anything? If so, what?

Do you like our evaluation sheet? Is it:
a. so good you want to keep it to show Mum?
b. better than a lamb roast?
c. something that should be framed and put in the Art Gallery?
d. plain bloody good?
e. a waste of a tree?

KATG: The language of your students is rather colloquial, to say the least.

LAT: I know. It's typically Australian. It would probably shock people of other nationalities, but it's the ordinary everyday language used and heard in Australian families all over the country — and, as I've already tried to point out, we are trying to operate as a family. Nevertheless, my students do know when such language is inappropriate. But you're leading me away from my main point, which was to illustrate that the more authentic writing tasks are the more writers will engage with them, and the more they engage the more effective they'll become as writers. Have I made myself sufficiently clear?

KATG: Perfectly clear, thank you. Please continue.

LAT: Our end-of-semester marking has taken on a whole new meaning and is even *pleasurable* because of the engaging variety of ways in which students now present their work. Performance may be a part of assessment if students so choose, such as Rachel's selection of songs in which she put language arts theory to music as part of her final assignment, cajoling even the footballers in her group to sing along in songs like this one:

[The Language Arts Teacher sings.]

> Day by day,
> Day by day,
> Oh, dear teacher, three things I crave:
> To know why I'm writing,
> To know who's going to read it,
> To know who really cares,
> Day by day by day by day . . .

KATG: You're not exactly Ella Fitzgerald, are you?

LAT: Did I ever claim I was? Have you read any Ella Fitzgerald picture books lately?

KATG: All right, all right, I didn't mean to upset you.

LAT: The song was meant to illustrate my general point about authentic literacy: I wanted to show how the anticipation of a real response alters — for the good — the commitment to a writing task. Because Rachel could picture her audience of peers and ached with caring over their potential response, she put her heart and soul into her assignment.

KATG: Very interesting. Now back to your baggage. Do you have anything else to declare?

LAT: Yes, I do: if it's all right with you, I'd like to take a look at a few of the different things people choose to write, and why.

KATG: Go ahead.

The Language Arts Teacher opens her briefcase and retrieves a sign saying "Rejoicing in Choices," which she shows to the KAGT.

KATG: "Rejoicing in Choices." I see.

LAT: A junior primary class in a small parish school wants the author of *Guess What?* to visit them. Innovating on the *Guess What?* structure of "Is she thin? Guess! Yes! Is she tall? Guess? Yes!" they send her the following irresistible invita-

tion in their own handwriting, with their own inimitable illustrations, in Big Book format:

> Guess what, Mem Fox?
> Not far away from you is a school called St.
>   Monica's.
> Is it small? Guess!
> Yes!
> Does it have children in Year Two who like to write?
> Guess?
> Yes!
> Do these children like your stories?
> Guess?
> Yes!
> Would these children like to meet you?
> Guess?
> Yes!
> Do they have some questions to ask you about
>   writing stories?
> Guess?
> Yes!
> Some people say you're far too busy to visit us but
>   guess what?
> We hope you're not!

Kim isn't writing clever innovations yet because he's only
five, but he is writing letters:

> *Dear men Fox,*
> *   Your aer a busybee and I like your books what you*
> *write and how do you change your hair colour?*
> *   Love,*
> *   Kim*

"Men" isn't the only one getting letters. Sue gets them, too. Dr. Susan Dauer was a 1991 American Fulbright scholar working with me at Flinders University. She and her fifteen-year-old daughter, Molly, arrived in late December 1990, and by mid-February Sue was dying for letters from the States. Had she and Molly been forgotten down under, or what? How was Gus the cat settling down in his foster home back there in Salem, Oregon? Didn't people at home realize she might be feeling a bit lonesome and in need of a little loving? Obviously not. One day Sue said to Molly, "Molly, if I don't get any letters in that mailbox tomorrow I'm going to cry." So Molly, grieving for her mom, wrote her a letter and posted it. She signed it "Arlis," the name of the friend back in America who was looking after the cat. The letter arrived, of course, on the following day:

> *Dearest Sue,*
>
> *I'm so sorry I haven't written for a long time. I know you get lonesome for someone back home. But there's sooo much to do, why would you be lonesome? You know everyone here thinks of you daily. We're jealous and envious of you (almost turning green). Don't waste your time thinking of us when there's a lot to do there. You know we think of you. That's plenty of thinking. Everyone here is fine. Gus is the usual. He's used to everything here. We'll hate to see him leave. Well, I'm sure you're busy so I won't keep you! We think of you daily!!*
>
> > *Love you tons,*
> > *Arlis*

Frank Halliday is a very different person from Sue and Molly, Kim, and the kids at St. Monica's. He's everybody's favorite janitor at my college. He has the sort of personality that inspires in people the confidence to spill out their secrets and joys, their hopes and their dreams, so he was one of the few to know, toward the end of 1990, how much I longed for my autobiography to be reviewed in the literary pages of the *Weekend Australian* newspaper. Each Monday morning we'd share my private anguish as weekend after weekend went by without reward.

(Months after the event I am about to describe, a favorable, if short, review did eventually appear in the *Australian;* it's also essential to know that there's a lifelike and therefore unflattering portrait of me on the cover of my autobiography, which is called *Mem's the Word* in Australia.)

At the beginning of January 1991 I went on my summer holiday. When I returned there was a mock-up of the *Weekend Australian* literary pages on my desk and, lo, a book review, written by beloved Frank himself:

Mem's the Word. **Penguin 173 pp. $14.95**

Dear Reader, may I first offer my apologies for not reviewing this book earlier. There are hundreds of books published in Australia each week and I made the mistake of judging *Mem's the Word* by its cover. After all, I thought, who would be interested in another book by some academic on an ego trip and then there's the author's mug on the cover! Not much going for it on face value.

The cricket was rained out one day so I found time to read it. Savour it would be a better description. Everyone has their own story to tell but only a talented few have the ability to share it with others

as Mem has done in this book. Her writing discipline
and word economy are obviously a product of her
many children's books. It encourages the reader to
see pictures in the mind, it involves us in the story —
everything a book should do. Please, please, read and
enjoy this book. It rivals *East of Eden*, on a smaller
scale of course.

If you see Mem Fox in the street don't stare and
fawn just because she is a great teacher and writer.
Give her cheek just to keep her feet on the ground,
e.g. "Mem we have something in common. I have
read your autobiography and you have red your hair."

                                        Frank Halliday

I chose to share these pieces in particular to try to begin
to illustrate a few of the vast number of genres we have to
choose from as writers. Only the *Guess What?* invitation was
written in a school setting; the others were intrinsically mo-
tivated outside school settings, and the level of affective engagement was high. Can we, I wonder, widen the opportunities
for the writers in our classrooms by offering them a much
greater variety of genres than currently exists? In some cases,
as we already know, a particular genre, such as the science
report, might need formal introduction, that is, a close inter-
rogation of that kind of text — its content, and its physical and
linguistic features — but many other genres are already understood and internalized.

We know, for example, that even three-year-old scrib-
blers understand genre: the form of their scribbled notes is
quite different from the form of their scribbled notices or
scribbled shopping lists. Perhaps writers need only a nudging

reminder of the variety of genres available to encourage them to write outside their normal rut.

An important feature of the genres I used as my examples was that none of them existed in a purpose/response vacuum. Frank might have looked at reviews on the literary pages to find out how to write his review; Rachel knew the requirements of songwriting; and Molly, Kim, Sean, and Stuart knew how to write letters. But none of them engaged in the writing for reasons that were not of great importance to themselves and their audience.

The power these writers had in common was knowing that different purposes do require different styles of writing and knowing where to go if they needed to study the features of a particular writing form. If we can provide this knowledge for the writers in our classrooms and the opportunity for them to use it for real purposes, it might provide a burst of educational adrenaline in our writing programs and add a whole new zing to our lives.

KATG: You may be right. So far, in any case, you haven't taken any wildly wrong turnings. I'm telling you this by way of encouragement.

LAT: Thank you. I have one last thing in my baggage. May I show you?

KATG: Of course.

The Language Arts Teacher opens her briefcase and retrieves a sign saying "The Return of the Affective," which she shows to the KATG.

KATG: "The Return of the Affective." I see.

LAT: A teacher — we will call her Mrs. B. — takes over a fourth-grade class, a day and a half before the class goes on a long-awaited excursion to the college at which I teach. She is the third teacher the class has had in ten days, thanks to the stupidity and blind inhumanity of the South Australian Education Department. It is particularly tragic for these children to have had such a transience of teachers since the adults in their private lives tend also to be rather transient. Mrs. B. grimly confides that the class is full of "monsters." She is clearly unhappy. She doesn't yet know the children, and she certainly doesn't like them.

As the children clamber into two buses, one of which I'm driving, I wonder if my college students will be able to handle them. One of my classes has been pen pals with this particular class over the last two months, and they're about to meet each other for the first time. There's to be a literary sort of performance by my students of stories, poems, plays, and songs, and then there's going to be a party — Yay! Fairy bread! Lamingtons! Chocolate crackles! Some of these little kids are so poor they're really hungry.

"Do you know Paula?" asks the child in the front seat, her eyes alive with excitement.

"Yes," I say, "she's really funny. Is she your pen friend?"

"Yes, an' I'm goin' to hug 'er."

Good, I think to myself. There's already a sweetness of spirit here, a sense of caring and being cared for. This child's heart is in motion as the wheels of the bus go round and round.

KATG: I hate to be pedantic, but everyone alive has a heart that's in motion. Please explain yourself.

LAT: Most of our educational aims and objectives focus on the cognitive corners of children's minds: the "how-to-know" bits, like learning how to read and write, like knowing about science, like learning how to do maths. Occasionally we remember also to focus on the physical aspects of children's education by providing opportunities for sport and fitness activities.

But in that old triumvirate of the development of the head, the hand, and the heart, which I remember being told about when I was in college, the heart — the *affective* aspect of education — is often ignored. Day after dreary day, particularly in high school, the mind is assaulted, the body moves, and although the heart does beat, which I don't deny, it remains largely un-*affected*. Curriculum-related joy, sympathy, laughter, excitement, jokes, longings, sighs of contentment, sadness, sorrow, anger, disappointment, and compassion are rare. Because all the emotions are readily available in stories, and stories are the most common foundation texts of literacy, they are supremely well-placed to provide what is currently lacking in the affective education of our students, but I'll develop that theme later.

I told you about the child on the bus because her heart had been *affected* for once in a curriculum-related activity, and I was thrilled. Have I answered your question adequately?

KATG: Yes, indeed. Please continue.

LAT: The buses arrive at the college. Tension drains the color from the face of poor Mrs. B. as her wild class tumbles down the steps in a riot of good-natured misbehavior. "Keep the noise down," she says. "Stay in line! Jamie! Natasha! Walk, please!" But her cries go unheeded. The kids are in ecstasy. I pat the hand of Mrs. B. "It'll be all right as soon as they're inside," I say. Her eyes roll.

It's dark inside the drama studio. The children can't see very well after the glare outside. Their hearts begin to pound. What will happen next? Flashlights guide them to their places, and the stories begin. "Once upon a time an old woman found a great big hairy toe in a forest, so she wrapped it up and took it home. . . ." The class is silent, rapt. Not a creature is stirring, not even a mouse. Not even Mrs. B., who is lost in the story.

The lights come on. Funny poems follow, and sorrowful poems, and still the wild kids sit and still the wild kids listen. And silly songs are sung and chanting books are chanted and the kids join in, and still the wild kids sit and still the wild kids listen. And then the final story is read: *Koala Lou. [The Language Arts Teacher reads the story.]* And still the wild kids sit and still the wild kids listen, but Mrs. B. is so *affected* by the story that she cries uncontrollably and has to leave the room: Mrs. B.'s mother is very ill and is unlikely to live.

Much has occurred in the half-hour performance: hearts have been given emotional nourishment arising from the curriculum; children have been enthralled; literature with its possibilities of words, structures, and rhythms has been heard and stored in the marrow of memories from where it might be borrowed later for writing or speaking; a sweetness of spirit has uplifted my students and their pen pals as they share the feast, chatting shyly, not quite knowing what to say; and the behavior of the wild ones has been exemplary, much to Mrs. B.'s astonishment and relief. (Perhaps that's why the Cree Indians call storytellers *magicians*.)

But best of all, Mrs. B. has been so personally affected, so connected to the magic of story in this half-hour literacy event that she will never be so misguided as to believe (if she ever did in the first place) in the possibility of developing literacy without literature. And she will never again think of literature merely as a tool for developing literacy, for she now understands *from the inside out* that literature provides essential sustenance for the soul: that it is of life and about life, and that classrooms lacking in literature are classrooms lacking in soul.

The depth of *affective* engagement in a story well-told or a book well-read is one of the priceless seeds of literacy, which, once grown, can be pruned and guided to spread in different directions based on personal needs and the needs of society. But if the literature seed is dried up or diseased — as it is in basal readers, for example — then the cultivation of literacy becomes a bruising, backbreaking business rather than a rewarding and heartfelt pleasure.

KATG: I presume that a darkened room and flashlights are not prerequisites for the development of literacy through literature. Most teachers teach in daylight and might find darkness difficult to come by.

LAT: Of course darkness isn't important! I think you're teasing me. I told that story because it is still vivid in my memory.

KATG: You say you "told that story. . . ." You have taken a great many stories out of your baggage. Why is that?

LAT: I used stories because stories connect us to our lives. I used stories because I thought you'd listen more willingly to stories than to sermons, lectures, or campaign speeches from the backs of bandwagons. I used stories because I grew up in Africa, where it was the custom to pass on culture and to teach through story, which I found to be a very powerful medium. And finally, I've been telling stories because once again I wanted to practice what I preach by adding an *affective* element to our dialogue. I hope I affected you a little since my stories were, in part, the means to that end. I wanted you to laugh and sigh and pay attention. Did you?

KATG: From time to time, certainly. Now if you would like to remind me of what you have been saying — in the form of a brief conclusion — I might allow you to pass. What were the four things you mentioned?

LAT: The Four *R*s, remember? Relationships, Reality in writing, Rejoicing in choices, and the Return of the affective. And I tried to weave them together using theory as my needle and stories as my thread. Now please may I pass? I'm drastically late for an appointment.

KATG: Yes, you may pass. You are free now to join the Language Arts Thinkers. I think you'll find they have been waiting for you.

[The Language Arts Teacher rushes toward another microphone and speaks rapidly to the Thinkers.]

Please excuse me for being so late. I was held up by the Keeper At The Gate. I had intended to give a formal presentation today, but there's no time for that now. Nevertheless, to us all — may old friends be found and new friends be made today; may this meeting of minds speak to the realities of our lives; may the choice we made to be present today cause us to rejoice and be exceedingly glad; and may our hearts be affected and our minds explode as we teach and learn together. Thank you.

7 Flashing Screens or Turning Pages?

Winning the War between Books and Television

Television will not go away. It's here to stay, and its attractions are many. One way of doing battle with it might be to get rid of it completely or to turn it off most of the time, but in most homes that would now be very difficult. Rather than wondering what we can do about television, we might as well focus on what we can do to make books and reading as attractive as watching TV. Why don't kids read? Let's start at the beginning.

Children learn to speak for many reasons, one of which being that they are completely surrounded by talk; they see it in action and they very quickly understand that using language produces excellent results. They learn to talk also because they badly need to: "Dink, dink!" they cry when they're thirsty. "Ganpa gone seepies," they whisper as Grandpa drops off to sleep. "My ball," they glower as a neighboring child steps forward menacingly. They observe the results of speaking and discover a million reasons to engage in the activity that is "talk."

In order to make books more attractive than television, we have to do with books what we have already done with talk. As adults we have shown that talking reaps rewards. We must do the same with books. We have to demonstrate that reading is as much fun as talking, and almost as necessary. We have to create in children a deep *need* for books; otherwise television will always win out. How might we do this?

When we look at the sort of home that produces book lovers, the first thing we notice — the most obvious, but strangely the most often forgotten, factor — is that such a home has books in it. There exist highly privileged children in our society who cannot read or will not read. It's not difficult to find out why: they have television; they have toys, computer games, personal VCRs, bikes, and all the other trappings of a well-off childhood; but they don't have books. These children often have a reading problem at school, which their panic-stricken parents disguise under the socially acceptable label of dyslexia. How can books become attractive if there aren't any books around to flick through?

The second essential factor in the making of eager, competent readers is that the children have books, and *bookshelves*, of their own so that favorite books can be owned and read over and over again. Ownership is important. I know of a child who read a particular favorite book until it was in tatters. His parents replaced it not once, but three times. Being able to own, and therefore able to reread, the book for years made that child into a reader.

The third necessity is a wide variety of reading material throughout the house — thrillers, paperbacks, magazines, newspapers, encyclopedias, classics, kids' novels, nonfiction books and manuals, specialist journals, and picture books. Some short books. Some long. Some hard for little children to read. Some really easy. As adults we do not read serious novels all the time — our needs vary, and we should remember that children's needs vary also.

The fourth requirement, I believe, is that children should be allowed to read whatever they want to read. At thirteen my own child was crazy about picture books — surely too young for her! And Jean Plaidy novels — surely too long for her! Once when she was bored at my sister's place she picked up, read, and loved *The Color Purple* by Alice Walker, which I would have thought was highly unsuitable for a child of twelve. However, because I wanted her to be a reader I allowed her to make the choices, and she became a reader.

The fifth essential factor is for parents to be seen to enjoy reading, which means reading in the daytime or early evening so that their children can watch the absorption in and enjoyment of books by their parents. I believe it's a fine thing to be seen to sniffle over sad books in front of children and a fine thing to delay washing the dog or getting to a ball game because a parent cannot put a particular book down.

The sixth necessity is that the books read by the children should be beautiful, intrinsically rewarding books such as *Where the Wild Things Are* (scary); *The Giant Devil Dingo* (how the world became); *Guess What?* (disgusting); *Julius, the Baby of the World* (hilarious); *Hop on Pop* (easy); and *Koala Lou* (touching). These beautiful books create a need by satisfying a need. If we didn't know chocolate was delicious we'd never crave it — so it is with books. These books all feel smooth, smell nice, look enticing, and present their readers with real rewards for the effort of reading them.

The seventh thing to be found in a book-loving home is that the parents usually take parenting seriously. They role-play parenting like mad. They know they ought to read to their children, so they do. The kids are caught up in a bookish world. At bedtime they are warm and safe with a big, loving, protective parent beside the bed reading them stories night after night. In the daytime they squeeze onto a comforting lap and in the security of a parent's loving warmth listen to all manner of horrors and joys coming out of books. The relationship between parent and child during the stories is one of warmth and love, which makes the child associate books with warmth and love and pleasure and security. How attractive books become!

And, finally, for children to be able to learn to love books they need **time** to read, a **quiet place** to read in, **warmth** in winter, **coolness** in summer, a **comfortable spot** to curl up in, and **enough light** to read by.

One of my small relatives was able to read but wasn't a keen reader and was dropping behind her classmates at school. I discovered that she wasn't allowed to read in bed. Amazing. She had a reading lamp in case she woke up in the night and was frightened. She had books on her shelves — I had seen to that. But she had no time to read; no quiet place to read in because the TV was always on; no warm place except bed because the warmest room had the television in it; and no comfortable sofa to curl up in because that was in the warm, well-lit, comfortable, noisy room that had the television in it! The mother's anxiety about her daughter's reading level was very real. She thought she had a big problem on her hands, but when the child was given the permission, the time, the books, the light, the comfort, and the warmth of reading in bed every night the problem was solved.

In the kinds of homes that produce avid readers, people still watch television but probably with discrimination. The child who loves books will gain enormously from watching television — much of the unknown world will be revealed, giving the child valuable information and insights to assist her later in her understanding of more demanding literature.

Let's now look at the attractions of television and compare them with a child's experiences in a nonideal school, for certainly such a school will drive schoolchildren away from books very quickly, straight to the channels of television.

First, television is watched by babies, partly because parents park them in front of it and partly because even babies perceive a *need* for TV to combat boredom. Is there such a thing as a TV readiness program? Of course not. Children watch television because it is intrinsically rewarding, because it's fun, and because it's worth doing.

However, in a nonideal school even children who can already read and who enjoy reading are put through a ridiculous reading-readiness program, sorting out this shape from that, coloring in from top to bottom of a page, following a pattern from left to right and so on. None of this creates a hunger for books. It creates boredom — so unlike the wonderful interest provided by television.

Children choose what they want to watch on television within the bounds of parental control. Research has shown that children actually prefer programs designed for adults, particularly comedy programs, and cops and robbers.

In a nonideal school there is no self-selection of books. Basal readers are provided, and everyone begins with reader no. 1 and grindingly slowly, ignoring any interests the children might have, progresses step by step to reader no. 157.

Television watching is not competitive. There is no such thing as a good television watcher or a bad one. No one has any idea about my capabilities as a television watcher — no one is better than I am, or worse.

But in a nonideal school every child knows who the best

readers are, and the worst. The reading scheme is so designed that the entire class knows that Katie is still on reader no. 10 in third grade; and Katie's shame pervades the classroom and alters her life by making her a public failure. No wonder she prefers television.

Television is fast, colorful, easy, funny, scary, informative, and slick. In a nonideal school with only basal readers the books look awful, the illustrations are banal, the plots and language are peculiarly uninspired; the content never makes kids cry or laugh or gasp or feel sick; the covers of the books aren't inviting; the size is predictable; the smell is off-putting. Often children can't be bothered to struggle with a reader because the reward in the end is not worth the effort — slow tedium, that's what basal readers provide. What a negative contrast to television!

Television can be watched in a warm and comfortable environment — on the floor, curled up in a chair, lolling on a settee, standing in front of the fire, and with others in the family watching the same program, enjoying the feeling of belonging and sharing as well as the content on the screen.

In a nonideal school reading takes place in a physically and emotionally cold environment, and in some discomfort. There is no sense of shared enjoyment and fun with books if a stern (but well-meaning) teacher is listening to a child trying to read a boring book and waiting, just *waiting* to pounce as soon as an error reaches her ears. In this situation the child associates books with fear, shame, and boredom. When did TV ever have that effect?

No one tells children that they must watch so much television per night because it is "a good thing to do." People watch it because it gives them pleasure. They need to watch it to relax.

Reading books, in a nonideal school, is often given for homework — a certain number of pages must be read and marked off on a bookmark by the following day. The child perceives no *need* to read except to be judged. Reading provides no pleasure and is anything but relaxing when the anxious teacher or parent barks out the correct word every time the child hesitates or guesses wrongly.

Television and books have one thing in common: it's what the child gets out of them that matters. Reading is not inherently good. Television is not inherently bad. What counts is the pleasure, the experiences, the relaxation, the growth in understanding, the satisfaction of need in each medium. I watch a lot of TV when I'm tired. During my vacations I never watch television — I read instead. Television doesn't answer my deepest needs on vacation. And long novels are too daunting to begin after an exhausting day of brainwork. Television and books have concurrent, different roles to play in our lives, but children who suffer at nonideal schools will only ever have TV because books have been made so deeply unattractive to them.

Book lovers who are fanatically and foolishly antitelevision forget that television is a marvelous medium for turning children on to books. While the BBC serialization of *The Secret Garden* was showing on TV the book was never on any of the shelves of libraries across the nation. I read Tolstoy's *War and Peace* as an adult only after watching three episodes on television: seeing the people helped me to sort out the complicated Russian names and made the book accessible.

Making books more magnetic than television is not quite as easy as turning a knob from On to Off. Nevertheless, if we could provide bookshelves crammed with a wide variety of attractive reading material, a loving, caring parent or teacher or two, and a school that looks and sounds like a loving, caring, book-filled home there would be more children who would love to read in spite of the flashing attractions of the television set beckoning from a different corner of the room.

8 | Conveying the Inexplicit

The Problem of Teaching What Can't Be Taught

In this chapter I'll be considering the rhythm of language and the choosing of words and their role in the development of powerful writers and speakers. I intend to explore the differences between merely "competent" writers and really "powerful" writers, and I'll be suggesting that competence can be taught whereas real power defies instruction.

Powerful communicators, as I've already said, understand intimately that the choosing of words and the placement of words has an *affective* impact on meaning — that response to meaning comes not only from minds but from hearts as well. They understand that words convey only a part of meaning and that the remaining meaning is conveyed by the rhythm of those words. I'm suggesting that writers who lack a sense of rhythm and a wide vocabulary may well be competent but will always be less effective than those who do have a sense of rhythm and know how to use it.

To demonstrate what I mean by "powerful" as against

merely "competent" communication, I will quote four powerful examples: first, Winston Churchill:

> We shall defend our island, whatever the cost may
> be. We shall fight on the beaches, we shall fight on
> the landing grounds, we shall fight in the fields and
> in the streets, we shall fight in the hills; we shall never
> surrender.

And from Thomas Jefferson and the American Declaration of
Independence:

> We hold these truths to be self-evident: that all men
> are created equal; that they are endowed by their
> Creator with inherent inalienable rights; that among
> these are life, and liberty, and the pursuit of happi-
> ness.

And from Shakespeare, out of the mouth of Mark Anthony:

> Friends, Romans, countrymen, lend me your ears;
> I come to bury Caesar, not to praise him.
> The evil that men do lives after them,
> The good is oft interred with their bones.

And finally, from the Bible (Matt. 5:2 – 12):

> 2. And he opened his mouth and taught them say-
>   ing,
> 3. Blessed are the poor in spirit: for theirs is the
>   kingdom of heaven.

4. Blessed are they that mourn: for they shall be comforted.

5. Blessed are the meek: for they shall inherit the earth.

6. Blessed are they which do hunger and thirst after righteousness: for they shall be filled.

7. Blessed are the merciful: for they shall obtain mercy.

8. Blessed are the pure in heart: for they shall see God.

9. Blessed are the peacemakers: for they shall be called the children of God.

10. Blessed are they which are persecuted for righteousness' sake: for theirs is the kingdom of heaven.

11. Blessed are ye when men shall revile you, and persecute you, and shall say all manner of evil against you falsely, for my sake.

12. Rejoice and be exceeding glad, for great is your reward in heaven.

As a delicious contrast to those magnificent words and their compelling rhythm, here's a quote from a basal reader:

"Today is Saturday," said Dick.
"Yes, it is Saturday," said Dora, "so we do not go to school."
"There is no school on Saturdays," said Mother.
"Jack and May will not be at school. They will be at home."
"Fluff and Nip do not go to school at all," said Dora.
"They stop at home and play."

"They stop at home and go to sleep," said Dick.
"Look, Nip is asleep now. Can you see him asleep,
  Mother?"

Any cognitive skills the writers of such prose are trying
to achieve are lost, I contend, due to the paucity of the vocabulary and the lack of a bedrock of rhythm that might capture children's hearts.

Because power exists within clearly defined, appropriate
boundaries, we do need to demonstrate and make available to
student writers a vast number of appropriate forms of writing
for different purposes, no matter how old or young they are.
They — and we — have to understand that there's more to
writing than writing stories.

In the last year, for instance, I've written all of the following and more: poems, lighthearted articles, job references, in-
structions, children's stories, persuasive public speeches,
autobiographical jottings, notes for the fridge, conference papers, academic texts, letters of complaint, phone messages,
letters of congratulation, advertisements, curriculum guide-
lines, letters of condolence, letters of thanks, my résumé, course
handbooks, responses to students' writing, letters to friends
and family, my tax substantiation report, information on ways
of improving writing, shopping lists, journal articles, and the
continuing chapters of an adult novel.

I couldn't have achieved that output without an inside
knowledge of the types of genres available and necessary for
each task. Through personal experience, by being taught, or
by asking for help I knew how to set out each piece, what
tone to employ, what the length should be, and what my readers
would expect.

However, understanding appropriate structures is only a

first step: structures are but useless skeletons until we have gathered a hoard of life-giving words and the knowledge of where best to put them. Can this be taught? That's the question.

The phenomenon of learning takes place in diverse ways, and we'd be fooling ourselves if we believed it happened only when we "teach" in the narrow sense. Of course it's possible to teach the punctuation of direct speech on a Tuesday and then to give a test on it the following Friday to gauge the effectiveness of our explicit teaching, but short-term success is no guarantee of long-term usefulness to the learner. I'm not suggesting that we should discount short-term success: without it long-term success would become an illusion. It's the guarantee of long-term success I'm wary about.

Our ultimate success as teachers can't really be measured until after our students have left us. If, in their continuing lives, our past students can deal confidently and competently with any real-consequences writing task that confronts them — then, and only then, can we claim to have taught them well.

If we have taught them to speak well and write well — by which I mean effectively — it's my hunch that a great deal of our teaching will have been inexplicit. It's impossible to "teach" all the words that powerful writers use. But if writers don't have a vast array of words to choose from, they discover they're disabled, gagged by ignorance. So where do our students acquire the wide vocabulary they need as communicators, if not through explicit teaching?

Similarly, it's impossible to "teach" a sense of rhythm, although many have attempted to do so through a deadly counting of beats and a noting of caesuras in lines of poetry. If writers (or speakers) *don't* have an ear for rhythm they'll place their words in any old order without realizing the danger inherent in such carelessness. I believe many children's books fail to become favorites not because the characters and plots aren't terrific but because they've been written by people who have no sense of rhythm. I also believe that many an angry memo fails to make its mark because it lacks the vicious rhythm needed to punch its message home.

The power of words, *the heat of meaning*, depends to a great extent on where words are placed. The heat of meaning cools if the rhythm doesn't feel right. So where do our students acquire the sense of rhythm they need as communicators if not through explicit teaching?

Both these problems, how to "teach" vocabulary and how to "teach" a sense of rhythm, have the same solution: by reading aloud or telling stories often and with expression. My passionate belief in the benefits of reading aloud will be perhaps best illustrated by a few stories.

I asked a school principal once if he could provide a group of children whose literacy seemed shaky and who might therefore benefit from what I had to offer. I also wanted to know privately whether anything I did could make a difference or whether I was just a hot-air educator. I wanted to test my own credibility. I was joined by my colleague Barbara Comber. Together we taught seven children, aged 9–12, twice a week.

Our assumption, backed up later by evidence in their writing, was that these children would need words to write with and that we would provide as many words as we could. We told them that we would do this, and why. "How can you write or talk without words?" we said. "The more words we have to choose from the easier it is to make people understand us."

We decided on our Tuesday visit of forty-five minutes to

read aloud or story-tell for ten minutes and then to focus on writing, and on our Thursday visit of thirty minutes to do nothing except read aloud a novel: *The Indian in the Cupboard,* by Lynne Reid Banks.

The long and the short of it is that we ended up spending the entire seventy-five minutes each week reading aloud *The Indian in the Cupboard.* I mention the minutes in detail because each minute was precious. These kids were at risk, after all, and we had very little time with them. Shouldn't we have demonstrated different forms of writing? Taught spelling? Engaged in so-called process writing? Assisted in the development of reading strategies? Drawn story-maps? Asked for retellings? Wasn't our credibility on the line? Weren't the principal, the teachers, the children, their parents, and we ourselves looking for *results?*

We made the decision to read the novel and abandon everything else because the plot was magnetic and the children were totally rapt in the outcome of each new development. I was watching little Stefan, one week, as Barbara was reading. His mouth was slightly open in an unconscious half-smile, and above his cheeks his black eyes were so full of happiness that I saw for the first time exactly what is meant by "His eyes were shining." Until that moment I'd thought it was a cliché, but no, Stefan's eyes were *alive* with shine.

Reading *The Indian in the Cupboard* did more for our group, we believe, than any itty-bitty activities we might have dreamed up, week by week. The plot was gripping, the writing style highly sophisticated, the vocabulary advanced and diverse, the sense of rhythm superb, and the characterization subtle. The book, as a satisfying whole, taught much more in our seventy-five minutes than we could possibly have taught without it. Reading it aloud meant that structures were heard rhythmically and, as such, would become part of the marrow of their understanding of how writing works. Reading it aloud meant new words were constantly being heard and learned in context, making it easier to guess their meaning.

So, when the principal, the teachers, the children, and their parents asked what we'd achieved, Barb and I replied with confident pride, amazed at our own courage: "We read a whole novel aloud. That is all." And when they looked at us aghast and said, "Is that *all?*" we didn't even blush. And when they said, "You mean you didn't teach them *anything?*" we said, "No, we didn't. But don't worry: *The Indian in the Cupboard* did."

The next story happened when I began to wonder about favorite passages of literature I'd heard read aloud and what effect they'd had on me. I remembered my English teacher reading Matthew Arnold's agonizing poem "Sohrab and Rustum" and how the whole class had been appalled that a father and son should mortally wound one another in battle, unaware of who the other was. I could remember only one line: "Truth sits upon the lips of dying men," so I browsed through my poetry books, hoping I'd find it.

I didn't find "Sohrab and Rustum," but I continued to browse until I came to a certain page, at which I turned to my husband and said, "*Now* I remember why I loved 'Ode to the West Wind.' It was on an old 78 RPM record when I was a kid, spoken by John Gielgud. I listened to it so often I almost knew it by heart. Listen, I can re-recreate his rendition exactly." And I read the verse that had caught my eye (Shelley is addressing the West Wind, herald of autumn):

> Thou on whose stream, mid the steep sky's
> commotion,

Loose clouds like earth's decaying leaves are shed,
Shook from the tangled boughs of Heaven and Ocean,

Angels of rain and lightning: there are spread
On the blue surface of thine airy surge,
Like the bright hair uplifted from the head

Of some fierce Maenad, even from the dim verge
Of the horizon to the zenith's height,
The locks of the approaching storm. Thou dirge

Of the dying year, to which this closing night
Will be the dome of a vast sepulchre,
Vaulted with all thy congregated might

Of vapours, from whose solid atmosphere
Black rain, and fire, and hail, will burst: oh, hear!

And then I wept: at the remembrance of it, at the sound of it, at its despair, and for the loss of my childhood. The words and rhythms of "Ode to the West Wind" remain in the marrow of my memory, not in the cognitive corners of my mind, able to be used whenever they're needed. Of course our teacher told us what it all meant, in explicit terms, but when I myself came to write it was the rhythm I needed and the rhythm I understood.

Having Shelley in my bones doesn't mean that I will write in his genre. I haven't written an "Ode to the North Wind," for example. The gains we make as writers, from hearing literature read aloud, aren't bound by form. Rhythm and vocabulary transcend form: they're tools of power that can be transported easily from one genre to the next according to our needs.

An understanding of the power of words combined with

the right rhythm makes me read aloud everything I write, apart from obvious things like shopping lists. I can now read aloud silently, in my head, although "reading aloud silently" sounds like a contradiction in terms. As I write this chapter, for instance, I hear every cadence, listen to every pause, and check every beat. I'm hoping that if you enjoy the rhythm of my words you might be inclined to like my content as well. If I *am* succeeding in pleasing you, where did I learn how to do it? Through explicit teaching? I doubt it. I learned it from hearing writing read aloud, wonderfully, and often.

Perhaps it was Shelley — but how will I ever know? — who guided me to the rhythm of the last line of *Wilfrid Gordon McDonald Partridge*: "And the two of them smiled and smiled because Miss Nancy's memory had been found again, by a small boy who wasn't very old either."

Whose rhythm — and how she could ever tell? — enabled Margaret Wild, in *The Very Best of Friends*, to produce these exquisite opening lines, with their commas and periods so precisely placed?

Jessie and Sam lived on a farm with fifty cattle, twenty chickens, four horses and three dogs. But there was only one cat. William. Sam liked cats but Jessie didn't. "Cats leave hair on the furniture," Jessie said. "Cats are silly, skittish creatures," she said. "Cats aren't nearly as useful as dogs," she said.

Perhaps Margaret Wild knew about rhythm because she'd once heard someone read aloud the ending of Oscar Wilde's *The Selfish Giant:*

"Who art thou?" said the Giant, and a strange awe fell on him, and he knelt before the little child. And the child smiled on the Giant, and said to him, "You let me play in your garden; today you shall come with me to my garden, which is Paradise." And when the children ran in that afternoon, they found the Giant lying dead under the tree, all covered with white blossoms.

How did E. B. White know exactly — and how can we ever *know* how he knew? — that he'd achieved a perfect choice of words and rhythm in the last lines of *Charlotte's Web*?

Wilbur never forgot Charlotte. Although he loved her children and grandchildren dearly, none of the new spiders ever quite took her place in his heart. She was in a class by herself. It is not often that someone comes along who is a true friend and a good writer. Charlotte was both.

And who helped Charles Dickens — could it have been Matthew, Mark, Luke, or John? And how can we ever find out? — to set his words in such a sad and satisfying order as he sent Sydney Carton to his death under the guillotine, at the end of *A Tale of Two Cities*?

It is a far, far better thing that I do, than I have ever done; it is a far, far better rest that I go to than I have ever known."

And moving from the sublime to the ridiculous (but still focusing on the rhythm of endings), which one — or was it many? — of the many beautifully crafted endings I've heard leapt across the boundaries and helped me to finish my long application for a senior lectureship in 1986?

> I have chosen, in this submission, not to recall my past history of employment conditions at the College about which I have been less than happy, because I wanted this document to be an entirely cheerful piece of writing, full of positive statements and high hopes. I want to look to the future, not to brood upon the past. The evidence is here. I rest my case. This, then, is my application for the position of Senior Lecturer in the South Australian College of Advanced Education.

Was it the rhythm that helped me to clinch my promotion? The question isn't entirely facetious. There were others that year who were as deserving as I was, whose applications were not successful. We learned later that, in a field of equally praiseworthy applicants, an ability to put words together had greatly influenced the panel. Jumping for joy, I thanked God, Shakespeare, and John Gielgud for their priceless gifts of words wrapped in a variety of rhythms.

In the cases I've just cited, I wondered where those writers and speakers had learned the variety of words they'd used and how they'd known where to place them for maximum effect. By reflecting on my own experience I know the information did not arrive in an envelope marked "explicit teaching." It came from the constant good fortune of hearing great literature beautifully delivered into my ear, and from there into my heart, and from my heart into my bones. It came from hearing plays performed, from hearing myself tell folk stories to children, from listening to Gielgud reciting Keats and Shelley, from listening to my teacher read "Sohrab and Rustum," from going to church and hearing the Sermon on the Mount, and from reading children's books aloud to my own child.

All this makes me wonder whether we, as teachers of writers, focus too much on the *mind:* have we forgotten, or did we ever know, the explosive power, the *necessity* of focusing also on the ear?

The grandeur of my examples so far — Shelley, Shakespeare, the Bible, and so on — may be creating the misconception that only the vast or the great in literature is worth hearing aloud. Not at all. There are implicit lessons to be learned from Dr. Seuss. The refrain in my book *Koala Lou* has the same four major beats as the refrain in Dr. Seuss's *Marvin K. Mooney.* His text says, "Marvin K. Mooney, will you please go now!" And my text says, "Koala Lou, I DO love you!" I ask myself what I would have done in that situation without Marvin. Fortunately I'd read the book aloud to my daughter over and over again and had remembered the phrasing for seven years. It was there, in my bones, when I needed it.

My focus has been on the acquisition of two powerful tools — rhythm and vocabulary — as a positive outcome of reading aloud. But surely the greatest good by far that comes from hearing language read aloud with love is enabling listeners to love literature, too: to hear books and stories and poems and applications for senior lectureships that they may never have heard before and may never hear again.

We need to ask whether education for literacy can occur solely through the mind. We need to wonder about the role of the *affective* as well as the cognitive, in learning to read or write anything. Are the bones and the marrow being left on the shelf? When we talk about the "basics" is it too much to hope that these are some of the questions that might be asked and answered to the lasting benefit of our children and their literacy?

In practical terms I am advocating — with passion, for all the reasons laid out in this chapter — the reading aloud of powerful literature in pursuit of the creation of powerful writers. Reading aloud is easy to do, unlike some of the assignments teachers are given; and from my observation it pays dividends in developing the literacy skills of writers of all ages.

9 | The Story Fights Back

Before I leap into the deep end of the particular passion of this chapter I might do well to make a couple of statements about how we teach language arts in Australia. First, we *claim* that we teach reading through the use of real literature, by which I mean through the use of trade books rather than basal readers. I guess we could say with a clear conscience that for the last fifteen years basal readers have been on the way out, even though classrooms still exist in which the method of teaching reading has remained unchanged and unchallenged since the 1960s. In spite of them I think we have reason to be proud of our standard of literacy, which, in the English-speaking world, is second only to that of New Zealand.

Second, we say we teach language arts through the "whole-language" method. But do we, really? There seem to be many definitions of whole language, so I'll clarify what I mean by that term.

My understanding of the term *whole language* is that it

developed in order to signpost a new way of teaching language arts in relation to an old way of teaching language arts: that is, by using language in wholes rather than by using language in parts. Our teaching used to be dominated by unreal language, and now (we hope) it's dominated by real language, which has *a real significance* to the person using it. This means our students are now reading and writing whole meanings for real reasons rather then messing about with unattached parts of language that have no real meaning or consequence on their own.

Real language implies real meanings — written or spoken — from real people to real people, for a variety of real purposes and real consequences. I prefer the term *real* language to *whole* language because it's explicit and easy to understand. Whole language, to my way of thinking, is nothing more or less than real language, and as such it will be with us forever.

There's a belief among many parents and teachers that children have to learn to read by reading unreal books before they're allowed to read real ones. By *unreal* I mean basal readers. In these basal readers the language is so unnatural it would be funny if it weren't so tragic:

> Mum got out of the car.
> The children got out too.
> They looked at the tyre.
> The tyre was flat.
> It was flat.
> "What will we do?" said Bill.
> "Fix it," said Jim. "Fix it."
> "Yes," said Dad.
> "You can help me fix it."

There's no fixing of that language. That language is flat. It is flat. The real language road is not traveled in such a book. No one in real life reads basals for pleasure. They provide only one pathetic reason for reading: words.

Basals aggravate the problem of the functionally illiterate because, frankly, they appear to have been written by the functionally illiterate. Johnny can't read — neither can Jenny — because faced with the dullness of a basal why on earth would they want to? Basals aren't even well illustrated: the eye is repulsed even before the heart and mind begin to be repelled.

Basal readers are emotional deserts between two covers. Little children who struggle across the arid vocabulary toward an illusive literacy often collapse along the way, thirsting for the language of life. They find themselves instead surrounded by death: a dead plot here, a dead theme there; a dead tone, dead setting, dead characters — everywhere a dead style. How pathetic to write any book, or to use any book, in order to teach merely the *mechanics* of reading. Real books offer the mechanics of reading as well as the emotional and intellectual mechanics of life itself.

Instead of constantly wondering *how* we should teach reading, I believe we should be asking *why*. Children exposed only to basals must wonder why they should bother to learn to read when what they read provides so little pleasure or fascination. There's no impetus to read when the rewards are so few. It's my suspicion that the use of basals in 90 percent of American classrooms is partly to blame for the frightening fact that the U.S. public school system graduates 700,000 functionally illiterate students per year while another 700,000 drop out.

On the other hand, real books — that is, trade books — give children many answers to the long-term question "Why read?" I'm talking about the sorts of books written by writers whom children love: Dr. Seuss, Paul Jennings, Roald Dahl, Margaret Mahy, E. B. White, Lois Lowry, Chris Van Allsburg, Katherine Paterson, and Kevin Henkes, to name a few randomly from among the many. Their books are funny and sad, outrageous and beautiful; they make kids *feel*, they provide information, and they're wonderfully entertaining.

That's my grand aim, too: to be as entertaining as possible. I try to touch the hearts of my readers. I hope I succeed in introducing them to the squealing delights and ineffable beauties of language. I hope I expand and explain their world. I hope my books make learning to read an easy and hysterical pleasure. I hope my choice of words, rhythms, and structures will help my readers to be powerful writers as soon as the need arises. I hope I strengthen the bonds between parents and very young children as they read together, giggling and yelling, whispering and sighing; and I hope I strengthen the bonds between children and books so they're seduced into loving reading *so* much that they'll be readers forever. And I aim quite openly to be a writer of popular books since writers without readers achieve precisely nothing.

When I read my books to children, what I want most from them at the end is a sigh of contentment because we have shared a little of life together. Such a sigh has never yet been heard at the end of a basal reader. The sigh is important. It's a signal that reading or listening to literature has been a deeply felt pleasure. It points to the possibility that reading might be rewarding again and again.

When I write for children, I put aside the notion of difficulty. I concentrate instead on joy and passion. I'm such a believer in the power of passion to get kids hooked on books that I always hope teachers will allow my books to stand alone for what they are, for they what say, and for what they contribute to the natural, joyful development of children's literacy. I weave a million little teaching points in and out of my stories to nurture accidental literacy — and to exterminate the need for any nasty, extrinsic, worksheet activities that some educational demolitionist might dream up!

My books have rhyme, rhythm, and repetition in them because, as a writer who happens also to be a teacher of language arts, it's second nature to know what's required for young readers. My great hope is that children will find a shortcut to literacy through my sneaky arrangements of structures, sentences, and words. I'm told — and it makes me very happy! — that many a reluctant reader has finally arrived at literacy by bouncing along the real-language road of *Hattie and the Fox*. I knew I was teaching when I wrote *Hattie*, but my first intention always was to produce — if I could — a great story, an irresistible work of art. Irresistible works of art, if we let the stories fight back, are excellent teachers of reading.

I was teaching again when I wrote that endearment I've mentioned several times: "Koala Lou, I DO love you!" The constant repetition of that line on page after page would, I hope, help children eventually to recognize those words through an emotional attachment to the story. *Koala Lou* is whole language. It has a meaningful connection to real life. The koala, if we dare to leave her alone, is an excellent teacher of reading.

I employed the same technique of repetition, but less obviously, in *Wilfrid Gordon*. The line " 'What's a memory?' he asked" occurs five times, making it five times easier to read than if it had occurred only once. The elderly people reply five times, using the same construction but a different term of address: " 'Something warm, my child, something warm.' ";

" 'Something from long ago, me lad, something from long ago.' " And so on. Each sentence is only half as difficult to read as it might have been since the first phrase is mirrored by the last: " 'Something that makes you cry, my boy, something that makes you cry.' " Kids soon cotton on to that. They're not stupid. Wilfrid Gordon, if we dare to leave him alone, is an excellent teacher of reading.

On the subject of Wilfrid, I once received a charming letter from a school summing up the success of their project on Mem Fox and her books:

> Thank you for the information and photographs sent earlier this year. They have been laminated and placed in our library for use in future years. The children were thrilled to hear from you and now regard you as a personal friend. With the interest stimulated by your response we were able to develop our "Author of the Month" into a ten week term theme across the curriculum. . . . *Possum Magic* and *Sail Away* were favourites, and our programme in self-esteem was boosted by *Wilfrid Gordon McDonald Partridge.* The many Australian flavoured stories lent themselves to much study of native animals, map-reading, capital cities and traditional Australian food. The beautiful illustrations fostered animated discussion. Your stories were the means of our children discovering books. They loved hearing them read aloud — not once but over and over. In fact, some now know the stories off by heart.

I was thrilled by the letter up to that point and had already pored over the photographs that had accompanied it:

photos of a *Possum Magic* party (excellent real language occurs at parties); a visit to an old-people's home (superb real language occurs between the young generation and the old); and a performance of *Hattie and the Fox* (a wealth of real language takes place in the planning and execution of performances). I felt excited that my books had been able to contribute in such a divergent way to these children's language development. However, the letter continued:

> We are enclosing copies of the programmes and worksheets used during this period, together with the photographs of the classes involved and some of the display. A grateful "thank you" from both of us.

Hyperventilating, I leafed through the pile of material that had been sent to me with so much professional pride and pleasure. My heart bled for the little souls whose journey along the real-language road had been so dangerously littered with rotten bits of language like this worksheet on *Wilfrid:*

Wilfrid Gordon McDonald Partridge
Mem Fox • Julie Vivas

Mrs. Jordan who

Mr. Hosking who

Mr. Tippet who

_____

Miss Mitchell who

_____

Mr. Drysdale who

_____

Miss Nancy who

_____

Who lost her memory?

_____

How old was Miss Nancy?

_____

Draw Wilfrid's memory objects:

Shells • Puppet • Medal • Football • Egg

And there was another one on *Hattie and the Fox.*

Hattie and the Fox
Mem Fox • Patricia Mullins

What did they say?

"   !" said Hattie.

"   !" said the goose.

"   !" said the pig.

"   ?" said the sheep.

"   ?" said the horse.

"   ?" said the cow.

Draw the fox jumping from the bushes.

In some classrooms this travesty passes for "writing." But it's unreal. It's parts of sentences only, not whole sentences. No one in real life fills in ditto sheets. Filling in the blanks doesn't foster fluency, higher-level thinking, or the creation of extended texts. Ditto sheets are nothing but the frustrating one-way streets of writing.

Anita Silvey, the editor of *The Horn Book* magazine, calls this appalling kind of exercise "the basalization of trade books" (September/October 1989). She says, and I cheer in agreement, "If literature in the classroom is to be effective teachers must learn to trust the book to do its own teaching." Let the story fight back!

The worksheets on *Hattie* and *Wilfrid* disturbed me for several reasons:

- They demonstrated a lack of trust in my books to do their own work.
- They bored children who had only just been hooked into books.
- There was no real communicative reason to write; that is, no meaning was passed from one person to another along a real-language road.
- In *Hattie and the Fox*, the recurrent line on each page is, "And Hattie said, 'Goodness gracious me!' " but the worksheet required the sentence to read, " 'Goodness gracious me!' said Hattie," thereby causing confusion and probably undoing the joyful repetitive learning that had already taken place.
- The age of Miss Nancy was/is irrelevant.
- The question "Who lost her memory?" demeaned the children's intelligence.
- And the sentences beginning "Mrs. Jordan who . . ." were

bad examples of English to set before children because when the blanks were filled in, as in "Mrs. Jordan, who played the organ," the meaning remained incomplete, in sentences without main verbs.

These exercises stole time from the writing of real English, for real purposes, for real people, for real responses with real consequences, in spite of the fact that the whole-language benefits of the earlier activities were wonderful and more than sufficient to develop the children's reading, writing, speaking, and listening skills. Why can't we leave books alone? If we want kids to love reading, we *must* allow stories to fight back.

At a conference in the American Midwest, I heard two teachers chatting together in line during a signing session. They'd had to wait quite a while, so they'd spent the time reading the books they wanted me to sign. As they moved nearer to me, one of them finished reading *Night Noises*. She turned to her friend and said, "Oh, isn't this book just darling? I can use it to teach the five senses."

For a start I couldn't immediately count five senses in *Night Noises*. Then I felt my heart contract with sorrow. What's so sinful about reading a book *for reading's sake?* Is there someone out there who's saying that reading a book in class has to be legitimized in some way — by using it to teach the five senses? If so, they're crazy and should be locked up for crimes against literacy. Dear God in heaven, protect me from these butchers! What's wrong with happiness as an outcome of reading? Is it too cheap? Too vulgar? What's wrong with laughter as an outcome? Or fright? Or enchantment? Or sadness?

My books have all these elements because I'm desperate for children to want to read. In *Wilfrid* Miss Nancy loses her memory; that's sad, but it makes kids want to read, and kids who want to read learn to read. In *Koala Lou* the main character howls her eyes out. In the about-to-be-published *Ben Again*, Ben's parents get divorced. In *Possum Magic* Grandma Poss makes bush magic. In *Sophie* Sophie's grandpa dies. Swans and peacocks kill each other in a war in *Feathers and Fools*. Scary nighttime noises haunt Lily Laceby in *Night Noises*. Is that a real witch in *Guess What?* And in *Hattie and the Fox* will Hattie outwit the fox?

A common element in these stories is that they don't put a pretty face on real life. I'm all for reality since children live in a real world and must face a series of real challenges every day. Life isn't all sugar — there's a lot of vinegar as well. By denying the vinegar in literature we provide bland, inoffensive, unappealing lies to children who know the truth. Basals tell the biggest lies of all. Lies don't make children want to read. Lies don't invite young readers inside the cover of another book, and another and another.

On the other hand, I do make sure that my books have happy endings. That final sentence — "And they all lived happily ever after" — provides readers with the possibility of a state of happiness, an essential longing fulfilled, so that even if their lives are wretched they will know that another sort of life *is* possible, and because it's possible they need not be crushed by despair.

"And they all lived happily ever after" is a literally fabulous last line, but it's found in so many stories around the world that we tend to take it for granted. Familiarity has bred contempt. We forget how essential it is. We forget how mind-blowingly reassuring it is. We no longer notice that it's trumpeting *four* pieces of great news in *one* simple statement:

"They *all* lived . . ." All, not one or two!

"They all *lived* . . ." They didn't die, they lived!

"They all lived *happily* . . ." Their quality of life was excellent!

"They all lived happily *ever after* . . ." This marvelous state of affairs went on and on and on!

It's an assurance that turbulence will be followed by calm. It's an assertion that happiness is possible, that love is everlasting, that good will prevail over evil, and that evil won't go unpunished. In spite of all the evidence to the contrary in our daily lives, this lovely line reassures us that we don't live in an entirely random, chaotic world. It presents us with a promise of balance and order, and it affirms a belief in the fairness of things.

I never use the actual words "And they all lived happily ever after" in spite of the fact that I'm very attached to them. I love their rhythm, their tone, their phrasing, and their sense of hope. They're perfect, but they're not mine, and I feel reluctant to borrow them. Instead, I hum the same message to a different tune.

It isn't only the message that's important in a last line — it's the rhythm and the phrasing. Words alone can't provide the reassurance that good will prevail — it's the placement of those words that's important: "And they *all* lived happily . . . ever . . . after." If the rhythm jerks or jars, so too will the sentiment. Readers and listeners need a calm and ordered rhythm in the last line to help them sail safely into port after all the storms and tempests they encounter in a story.

Trying to achieve this calm and ordered rhythm is a nightmare. I throw off my writing persona and become a musician instead, beating out possible rhythms with my finger, talking aloud, fumbling for words, and attempting to find a tune that will fit them. Mark Twain said the difference between a right word and an almost-right word is as big as the difference between a lightning bug and lightning — but I didn't need him to tell me that. It can take days for a pause to appear at exactly the right moment in a final sentence, for a word to be found with two syllables not three, for the beat of the meaning to be aesthetically correct, for the restoration of peace after chaos.

Even in the finale of my autobiography, written for adults, I tried to convey the rhythmic hope inherent in a happily-ever-after ending:

> Right now my life is at the height of its summer and I'm reveling in it, grateful for its fruits. In the winter of my days, when these green memories lose their leaves and wither, I imagine I'll turn the pages of this book and marvel at my good fortune, wondering if I exaggerated here and there since there's so much mention of sunshine and so little mention of rain. Outside my window a kookaburra sits on an old gum tree laughing in the gathering dusk, celebrating with me this high summer. The book is written. We're feeling on top of the world, the kookaburra and I.
>
> Yet the story continues. The ending is not The End.

Neither did I forget, after the crescendo of tension in *Hattie and the Fox*, to put a few crumbs of comfort in that conclusion:

> And Hattie said, "Goodness gracious me!
> I can see a nose, two eyes, two ears, a body, four legs,

and a tail in the bushes! It's a fox! It's a fox!" And
she flew very quickly into a nearby tree.

"Oh, no!" said the goose.

"Dear me!" said the pig.

"Oh, dear!" said the sheep.

"Oh, help!" said the horse.

But the cow said, "MOO!" so loudly that the fox was
frightened and ran away. And they were all so surprised that none of them said anything for a very long
time.

Even in *Guess What?*, a very brief book, I felt I couldn't
leave children in the state of mock fear that Vivienne Goodman and I had created through my words and her incredibly
brilliant illustrations. I had to say, in my own way, in my own
words, "Look, kids, it's okay. This old woman is just fantastic.
She isn't scary at all! She's wonderful!" The book ends with
my indulging in a literary hugs-and-kisses-conclusion yet again:
"Some people say she's really mean, but guess what? She's
NOT!" So although I never actually say, "And they all lived
happily ever after," I mean it, every time.

I guess in a way I love my readers and care about them,
even though I don't know them. I care enough to build a
shelter with my words, a safe haven from the storms of life.
When my readers knock on the door, I let them in and close
the door. I wrap them snugly in the warmth of fiction. Then
I lead them to the window, and together we gaze at the world
of the book. We watch storms raging. We see mists of death
and danger. We see fogs of divorce and disappointment. We
gasp at wars and turn our faces from cruelty. We see the elderly lost and confused. We see children distressed. We weep
with sadness and tremble in fright, but it's all right — we're

together at the window and we're looking after each other in the warmth of our safe haven.

Then the clouds roll away. The end of the book is in sight, and we can see forever. We watch vanquished foes sneaking off toward the horizon. We watch with approval as a flurry of activity restores order to the world. We see the smiles of heroines and heroes, and we hear their cheers. We witness with relief the reestablishment of happiness, the righting of wrongs, and the triumph of love.

The last line is spoken. I open the door of my shelter, and the sun bursts in. As I say farewell to my readers, I know that they leave me having learned a little of life. They're more prepared to deal with the world because of what they've seen through my window.

In these stormy times when banks are collapsing; farmers are going broke; trade wars and real wars are being waged; refugees are breaking their hearts and ours; the discontented and dispossessed in our cities are protesting; investment is falling; and inflation, the deficit, and unemployment are rising — how much more can we stand? — we need stories for our times with sunshine in the last lines. I hope I'll be able to write them; and if I succeed in doing so, I hope the stories will be able to fight back.

10 | Once upon a Time There Were Three...

The brain plays an important role in learning to read. In this chapter, however, I'd like to deemphasize the brain for a while by focusing yet again on the heart and the role that emotional factors play in the development of literacy. I'll be concentrating on intangible, *affective* influences on reading because I believe it's time someone stood up and told those miserable, measurable, cognitive factors they've had more than their fair share of our time for years, with precious little to show for it other than an appalling level of illiteracy and a high level of cultural ignorance.

As a storyteller I know that all the best stories go by threes, which is fortunate in this context since I'll be wearing three hats as three different people: the mother-as-writer, the teacher-as-writer, and the compulsive-shopper-as-writer. The factor of three will also appear as I explore the revealing relationships between the child, the adult, and the book, whenever they meet in the act of reading.

I'm certain that learning to read and learning to love reading owe a great deal (much more that we ever dreamed) to the *nature of the human relationships* that occur around and through books. If we could sneak into the homes of avid readers, I think we'd discover very often that the comfortable relationship between an older reader and a younger reader during the shared reading of a mutually loved book might be a key factor in the child's success.

On the other hand, if a child were experiencing difficulty in learning to read, we might discover a difficulty in the nature of the relationships between the child, the older reader, and the books they were attempting to read together. Unjust though it is, we tend to lay all the blame on children when they fail to become readers. We call them "reading disabled" or "learning disabled," whereas "teacher disabled," "text disabled," or "relationship disabled" might be more apt in the circumstances.

We should not be surprised when children don't learn to read or to love reading: Consider the quality, or lack of it, in the type of texts they have to read in school. Consider the boredom, the irritation, the impatience, and the tension created between parents and children, and teachers and children, as an inwardly sweating child attempts to decode a deadly basal reader. Consider the hostility in many homes. Consider the frightening coldness of those teachers and librarians who believe that correct teacher behavior is to be formal and aloof; who believe that classes might run riot if the children discovered their teachers' first names; who rarely laugh in the classroom and would rather die than cry in front of the children; who allow no room for any kind of comfortable, amused, or relaxed relationship with young children learning to read. Why are we so foolish as to expect children to learn to read if

they're tense, unhappy, and fearful? Did we ever learn anything in such an atmosphere?

All this and more troubles me whenever I sit down to
write for children. Writing is a complex affair at the best of
times, but the responsibility of creating texts that might or
might not create avid readers becomes an extra burden. I have
to aim to please parents, librarians, and teachers without dis-
pleasing children; I have to try to engage children without
boring adults; I have to attempt to instill my own homespun
values — for what they're worth; and I have to try to raise the
level of literacy and cultural awareness of my readers all at
once, within the confines of a thirty-two-page picture book.
It's difficult, but I'm encouraged to keep trying by focusing
my attention on a specific picture in my head.

When I write I don't see the illustrations in the story.
They are crowded out by the picture of what might happen
after the story is written. I visualize a scene in an ideal world:
a child in bed, a parent on the bed, and my book open between them. I see interconnecting relationships threading them
all together to make a loving circle. I see the child relating to
the book. I see the parent relating to the book. And through
the book — my book — I see the child and the parent relating
to each other.

As a mother, I believe the most important of these three
relationships is the relationship between the parent and the
child. Again and again I find myself writing with the specific
purpose of heightening and making explicit the affection between parents and children. I write so that parents who find
it hard to put their love into words can nevertheless express
their love through *my* words. In my mind's eye I see my stories initiating cuddles and romps at bedtime; I hear my words
creating kisses and laughter; and I hope that my endings will

contribute tenderness to that last good night. One of the clearest examples of myself as mother-writer is *Koala Lou,* in which a mother's love is reassuringly portrayed as constant, no matter what.

But I'm a teacher, too. As a teacher, I believe the most important relationship is the one between the child and the book. I try, as a teacher-writer, to write energetically to capture attention. I try to write rhythmically and repetitively to ensure that my words dance inside the child's head long after the story is finished. I try to use touching, crazy, scary, rowdy themes that will deliver an appropriate meaning to my young reader without my preaching or talking down. I try to use the best words I can find, the most exciting words — words like *squint, peek,* and *peer* in *Night Noises* — in case my book is the only one my young reader will ever own. I try to write so the gorgeous little kid in my head will experience, as she reads, a range of emotions from heartbreak to elation, because she must *feel* something in order to want to return to the book. If she does return to my book over and over again, she'll teach herself to read (although her parents will of course take the credit for her accelerated progress and boast about it at dinner parties). Above all I try to write in such a way that I will, I hope, attract the child lastingly to literature. *Hattie and the Fox* seems to provide some of these ingredients. It's the sparks in the relationship between a child and a book that create the fire of literacy. As a teacher-writer I live in terror of turning children off books by writing, as it were, with damp matches.

As a compulsive shopper (and this will appear frivolous although my underlying intention is serious), I believe the most important relationship of the three between the child, the parent, and the book is the one between the parent and the book, because if parents don't buy it, how will I be able to maintain the income level to which I've become accustomed?

Before hands are thrown up in horror at this sordid talk, let me say it's no bad thing for parents, for children, or for my publishers that I have a continuing concern about the health of my finances since it forces me to write more carefully than I might have written had I been born an heiress to the Rothschilds' fortune. It forces me to lift my game. It forces me, in a book as short as *Koala Lou*, with only 410 words, to rewrite the story forty-nine times, over two years. It forces me to write ostensibly, but not exclusively, for children since I know that if children are to have the chance to read any of my books I have to place an emotional magnet within my books in order to attract the adults clutching the credit cards.

For this reason I'm always thrilled when men and women whom I've never met before and may never meet again hold me by the wrist, look deep into my eyes, and say, "I want you to know my favorite book of all time is *Wilfrid Gordon McDonald Partridge*. I still can't read it without crying." The trembling stranger is telling me, at least in this instance, that I have written well for adults. Having written well for adults means the book is indeed being bought by adults. This in turn means children have had a chance to read it and judge it for themselves.

Having looked at what goes on in *my* head as I write, let's now take a look inside the head of someone who writes basals. We need a name for him, so we'll call him Basal Bill.

When Basal Bill sits down to write, he doesn't have any relationships in mind, let alone three. His books don't gather parents and children into a circle of love because there's no room for love in his dreary prose. Poor old Basal Bill is seized by the mistaken conviction that books aimed at young readers should be carefully drill-and-skill-graded in terms of word choice (keep 'em simple), word length (keep 'em short), word type (keep 'em in their word families), and choice of theme (keep 'em bland in case kids get distracted by the story and forget to focus on the see-Spot-run vocabulary). Basal Bill earns full marks for creating tedium, tension, and terror. He also gets ten out of ten for turning kids off books so fast that, as I write, millions of illiterates are shaming the nation and, more sadly, shaming themselves.

Basal Bill, allow me to tell you a story. I have always been a working mother, which is another way of saying I've always been a guilty mother. When my daughter, Chloë, was a child, she and I used to set aside a day in both her spring and autumn holidays just to hang loose together: Special Days we called them. She'd choose the activities and present me with the plans. On one of these occasions she decided we should take a picnic to a museum called the Pioneer Village. She was five years old. We unpacked our picnic on the porch of the old schoolroom.

"What's for afters?" said Chloë.

"Afters?" I said. "You shouldn't be thinking of afters till you've eaten what comes before."

"Well," she said, "one must sustain oneself."

"I beg your pardon?" I said.

"One must sustain oneself. You know, like Winnie-the-Pooh."

From that day on "One must sustain oneself" entered our family vocabulary and is most frequently used when one of us is on a diet and is caught raiding the fridge: "It's all very well," says the guilty person, "but one must sustain oneself!" With this famous line Winnie-the-Pooh regularly creates and re-creates a literary and emotional togetherness in our family.

The trouble with you, Basal Bill, is that you have no such fun in your barren life. You aim for the dirt. Look up! Aim for the moon. You'll surprise yourself. Right now you're wildly underestimating the capabilities of young readers to grasp an astonishingly high level of vocabulary when it appears in a story that really appeals to them. They won't find it difficult to read "One must sustain oneself" because if they *adore* the story they'll ask for it to be read over and over again. And the adult reader will love the story, too, because a real writer wrote it with an adult as well as a child in mind. And joy will surround the shared reading of that book, to the lasting benefit of the child and her literacy, let alone her emotional health.

Since when have you considered the emotional health of a child, Basal Bill? And how about the damaging effect your writing has on adults, Bill? Have you ever thought of that? Have you ever considered how you turn *teachers* off reading, let alone kids? Why can't you get it into your head that *adults* have to love books before kids have a chance to love to read them? Enthusiasm is infectious, Bill! Don't you sometimes ask yourself why your distasteful texts aren't shared in youth and remembered into old age?

Let me tell you another story. Tom Bernagozzi is an insanely hardworking and gifted teacher in Bay Shore, New York. He teaches third grade. Once a month he sends me his class magazine, *The Times of 3 Be*. In one edition many children's authors and other public figures shared with his class their favorite childhood reading material. I hate to tell you this, Bill, but your books didn't shape up for a mention, and I think I know why.

Cynthia Rylant and Eric Carle listed comics as their favorite reading. Cynthia's comics were of the "mushy" variety; Eric's were funny and heroic: Mickey Mouse and Flash Gordon. Now why didn't you ever think of writing things that were mushy, Bill? And where's the humor and heroism in your dry prose? Emotional stirrings help to bind kids to reading in a splendid relationship that creates literacy. Look to it, Bill! It's never too late to start.

Bill Martin Jr and Steven Spielberg listed *Treasure Island* as their favorite book. If they were like me, as kids their hearts nearly stopped beating when the cane of the menacing blind pirate, Pew, kept tap, tap, tapping through the opening pages. I can't remember my heart ever registering a single lost beat reading a basal reader. It's the lost heartbeats that grab a reader, Bill, not the emotionless monotonous beats in Dick-and-Jane.

Trina Schart Hyman and Senator Edward Kennedy wrote that their favorite book was *Lad: A Dog*, by Albert Payson Terhune. I had never heard of it, but according to Trina she got into all the Albert Payson Terhune stories: "They were always sad at the end," she said, "but I loved them anyway." I've never read a sad ending in a basal, which means the writers of basals have been missing out on a great device for hooking kids into books.

Do you have some sort of problem with sadness, Basal Bill? Do you think crying is bad for reading development? I'd say boredom was worse. *Charlotte's Web* has a sad ending, but it's one of the most popular children's books of all time. Children relate to it. Adults relate to it. Adults and children relate to each other through it. People of all ages cry buckets over it, and it sells and sells and sells. I love it so much myself I've already asked for the last lines of *Charlotte's Web* to be read out at my funeral.

If I searched from now till kingdom come, would I ever be able to find an ending in a basal reader that was sufficiently exquisite to be read out at my funeral? The notion is ridiculous. Writers of basal readers don't need to write as beautifully as E. B. White. They have no pressure to write well enough to impress the adult with the credit cards because school districts, in their sad, mad ignorance, will buy them anyway. More horrifying is the fact that if the schools don't provide the basals, parents will often complain! Can't they see that basals are toxic to literacy? Why would anyone want to feed kids poison in a land abundant with nonpoisonous nourishment? Enlightened teachers have an urgent task: to enlighten parents as well.

Judy Blume's best-loved, nontoxic book as a child was Ludwig Bemelmans's *Madeline*. In *The Times of 3 Be* she stated:

> When I was small my mother took me to the public library in Elizabeth, New Jersey, where I would sit on the floor and browse among the books.
> . . . My favorite was *Madeline* . . . I loved that book! I loved it so much I hid it . . . so my mother wouldn't be able to return it to the library. Even after the overdue notices came I didn't tell my mother where the book was. If only I had asked I'm sure she would have bought me my own copy but I didn't know that was a possibility then. I thought the copy I had hidden was the only copy in the whole world. I knew it was wrong to hide the book but there was no way I was going to part with *Madeline*. I memorized the words in the book and though I couldn't really read I pretended that I could.
> It's more than forty years since I hid that copy of *Madeline* and I've never done that again, but I can still recite the story by heart. And when my daughter was born *Madeline* was the first book I bought for her. . . . Some books you never forget. Some characters become your friends for life.

Can anyone conceive of a child loving a basal enough to
hide it away for safekeeping? Can anyone conceive of a visit
to Paris being enhanced by the text of a basal reader? I wonder how Judy Blume felt the first time she found herself in
Paris. Did she remember that Madeline lived there? Did she
hope to meet her, in her heart of hearts? We happened to be
in Paris when Chloë was six. She, too, loved *Madeline* to dis-
traction: "In an old house in Paris that was covered with vines
lived twelve little girls, in two straight lines."

As we walked toward the Eiffel Tower, we saw an old
house, all covered with vines. Chloë's eyes popped.

"Is that where Madeline lives?" she asked, in awe.

"Of course," I said, without pausing or blushing.

Even my husband pretended I might be right. On that
cold winter's morning the excitement of being so close to
Madeline warmed our hearts. We drew closer as a family as
we shivered and shared and wondered together, outside her
house. Madeline lived! Good grief!

When children love books they want to own them, to
keep them forever, so the memories and relationships sur-
rounding the book never fade. We still have a treasured copy
of *Madeline* although my little wide-eyed kid in Paris is now
an adult.

I recall attending a Christmas function, once, at a local
bookshop. A parent and a four-year-old child presented a tat-
tered copy of *Possum Magic* to be signed. The child looked
anxious and even grumpy. His embarrassed parent whispered,
"Robbie didn't want to come this morning. We told him *Possum Magic* was your book, and he's terrified you'll want it
back. It's his most treasured possession." *Possum Magic* had
become this child's equivalent of *Madeline*. I grinned from ear
to ear.

Susie, the niece of one of my friends, loved *Hattie and the Fox* so much it wasn't she who hid the book away but her mother, Margaret, who had read it aloud so often she could say it in her sleep. Can anyone conceive of a parent knowing a basal by heart? Margaret knew if she had to read it one more time she'd go around the bend, so she "lost" the book for a while on the top of a cupboard.

It came back into family circulation when Susie's little sister, Linda, was ready for it. Margaret always read the next-to-last page at the top of her voice: "But the cow said, 'MOO!' so loudly that the fox was frightened and ran away." Linda pretended not to appreciate her mother's dramatic efforts. At only two years of age she could predict exactly when that page was coming and would put her fingers in her ears and say, "Don't read that page! Don't read that page!" Yet she wanted the book read over and over again. Half the fun of it was calling out, "Don't read that page!"

Parents, teachers, and librarians must get to know the books currently available for children — especially the available books that children absolutely *adore*. It's one of the most important tasks we have in the development of literacy. Next we have to make these books casually available and to trust that, given the freedom to choose, children will pick them up and read them with enjoyment. We have to note, along the way, that some books *supposed* to be for children please adults without pleasing kids. As we all know, award-winning books beloved of adult critics sometimes die in the hearts of children.

In Australia, Paul Jennings, one of the most popular writers for children, has never won an adult-awarded prize. Fortunately his readers are old enough to buy their own books or at least to demand that the books be bought. Many a reluctant reader has been rescued from illiteracy as a result of his deceptively simple, hilarious texts. His popularity among Australian children surpasses even that of Roald Dahl, and he's probably on intimate terms with the entire Rothschild dynasty by now!

An adult who does bless the existence of Paul Jennings's books is Pam Romanis, a student of mine who wrote the following in an assignment:

> My son often says to me, "Why do I have to learn to read? I won't need that to be a BMX champ."
>
> I can't help but feel that somewhere along the line both his teachers and his parents have failed to get the point across to him.
>
> "Reading," I tell him, "is useful in everything you do: to learn more about the things you are interested in; for sheer enjoyment; and because there is information everywhere around us which we *need* to know."
>
> I think we are reaching him at last. It was a moment of great joy to walk into his room and find him sitting on his bed reading a Paul Jennings book. I just held my breath, not wanting to interrupt the moment. After calmly walking out of his room I charged down the yard, grabbed Ken around the waist and screamed out, "He's reading! He's on the bed reading!"
>
> That's what I am going to love about teaching.

One of the most moving letters Paul ever received was from a teacher in a hospital-school. One of her students was a girl who had been badly burned and was in great pain. She had been in hospital for three months. One day her father was on one side of the child's bed and her teacher on the other, reading from a typically funny Paul Jennings story. At one point the girl's face cracked into a smile, her first smile for three months. Her father was so happy he wept. Such is the power of literature, which no basal can ever hope to achieve.

When ordinary readers, such as parents, share books with children within a connecting circle of love, they have no overt teaching in mind. They do not have a list of behavioral objectives folded away in the back pockets of their jeans. They don't hold up the cover of *Possum Magic* and say, "Now look at the cover and tell me what you think this book might be about." They don't ask how many little girls there were in the story of *Madeline*. When little kids stumble over a word, parents just tell them what the word is, without fussing. They don't mind, up to a point, reading the same book many times if the child is still deriving enjoyment from it. They don't get tense when their children claim they can read the books themselves and struggle to do so, incorrectly. They accept that by-heart reading is the cradle of reading competence, and they celebrate it with amusement whenever it occurs.

Of course there are teachers in increasing numbers who recognize the value of real literature and who recognize also the enormous importance of establishing relaxed familylike relationships within their classrooms. In such classrooms children are protected from the toxicity of basals and are instead given the time to read real literature and the freedom to choose their own books. And they are trusted to react to their reading in their own manner.

On a recent visit to Sydney I found myself in a classroom literally humming with real literature. Eight-year-old Carina (not her real name), a middle-class, angelic-looking but tragically abused child, had written and composed a song in my honor, inspired by many readings of *Koala Lou*. It had been entirely her own idea. A teacher had noted down the tune so she and Carina could teach it to the class, and a poster of the words hung on the wall. In the special visitors' chair I sat expectant, and waited.

Carina took up her baton and, pointing to the first line, steadied her trembling hand. The music started, and the children sang such a sweet song about the absolute constancy of mother-love I wanted to lie on the floor and abandon myself to sobs.

> Koala Lou, I do love you!
> I always have.
> I always will.
> So don't be sad,
> Please do not cry.
> You know I love you
> For you are my child.
> Koala Lou, don't you cry!
> Be glad, be happy,
> My Koala Lou.
> Koala Lou, I do love you!
> I always have
> And I always will,
> My Koala Lou.

A book (one of *my* books!) had been the means of binding the whole class together. Makeup ran in black rivers down my face. I was a mess.

In closing I will once again wear my three hats simultaneously: my mother hat, my teacher hat, and my compulsive-shopper hat. As I wrote the story that will end this chapter, I longed to forge three loving relationships through my words: I wanted a lively child to be lulled into rest through a hypnotic and protracted attraction to the repeated words and rhythms in the book; I wanted tired parents to love me, and love the book, for its calming qualities; and I wanted to make it possible for parents and children to relate warmly and gently to each other at the end of the day (when both parties are often fraught with tension and tears) as they named together the different animals in the pictures. It's called *Time for Bed:*

> It's time for bed, little mouse, little mouse,
> Darkness is falling all over the house.
>
> It's time for bed, little goose, little goose,
> The stars are out and on the loose.
>
> It's time for bed, little cat, little cat,
> So snuggle in tight — that's right, like that!
>
> It's time for bed, little calf, little calf,
> What happened today that made you laugh?
>
> It's time for bed, little foal, little foal,
> I'll whisper a secret, but don't tell a soul.
>
> It's time for bed, little fish, little fish,
> So hold your breath, and make a wish.
>
> It's time for bed, little sheep, little sheep,
> The whole wide world is going to sleep.
>
> It's time to sleep, little bird, little bird,
> So close your eyes, not another word.

It's time to sleep, little bee, little bee,
Yes, I love you, and you love me.

It's time to sleep, little snake, little snake,
Good gracious me, you're still awake!

It's time to sleep, little pup, little pup,
If you don't sleep soon the sun will be up!

It's time to sleep, little deer, little deer,
The very last kiss is almost here.

The stars on high are shining bright —
Sweet dreams, my darling! Sleep well, good night!

11 Men Who Weep, Boys Who Dance

The Gender Agenda between the Lines in Children's Literature

During a rambling children's literature tutorial in 1978, I was startled into attention by something my professor was saying. Had I heard correctly? That 85 percent of the main characters in stories for children were male? That girl characters rarely did anything — rather they had things done to them? That sexism was clearly rampant, even at a quick glance of a dozen randomly selected books? Good grief, I thought sanctimoniously, if I wrote children's books I wouldn't be so sexist. Famous last words.

Remembering the 85 percent statistic, I asked my own undergraduate students to write the beginning of a children's book and to read it to the class. Most of them chose to make their main character male. When I asked if their character could be female instead — without ruining the aim of the story — they were puzzled to realize that this was absolutely possible and wondered why they hadn't thought of it, given the heightened awareness we have toward sexism in the so-called liberated world we now live in.

We discussed the invidious nature of sexism in literature and how quietly it conditions us into certain accepted, unquestioned ways of seeing and reading the world. I told them of the hundreds of letters I receive each year from devoted fans of *Possum Magic,* many as young as five, who are already so deeply conditioned into sexist expectations of literature that they say, "I love Hush. I love it when he gets invisible," in spite of the fact that Hush is definitely female. The word *she* appears rhythmically and repetitively, early in the story:

> Because she couldn't be seen, she could be squashed
> by koalas.
> Because she couldn't be seen, she could slide down
> kangaroos.
> Because she couldn't be seen, she was safe from snakes
> which is why Grandma Poss had made her invis-
> ible in the first place.

It's alarming to consider that by five years of age children mentally enforce a sex change in a literary female protagonist because they find the idea of an active, interesting, self-respecting female main character simply unthinkable.

Gender stereotypes in literature prevent the fullness of female human potential from being realized by depriving girls of a range of strong, alternative role models. I believe that male human potential is also stunted by such material. Everything we read, from sexist advertisements and women's magazines to romance novels and children's books, constructs us, makes us who we are, by presenting our image of ourselves as girls and women, as boys and men. We who write children's books, and we who teach through literature, need to be sure we are opening the doors to full human potential, not closing them. We have the power to change "gender-appropriate" behavior and attitudes, yet many of us seem blind to the opportunity.

Girls can do anything, or so we are told. They can be anything. They can feel anything. Why is it, then, that in children's literature they are still portrayed more often than not as acted upon rather than active? As nurturers rather than adventurers? As sweetness and light rather than thunder and lightning? As tentative, careful decision makers rather than wild, impetuous risk takers? Could children's literature be partly to blame for the fact that we grown-up girls have been denied in our womanhood the excitement and power so readily available to boys and grown-up boys?

Let's flip the coin for a moment. Boys can do anything, too, and be anything, and feel anything, or so we have assumed. Why is it, then, that they aren't allowed to cry? Why is it that ballet dancing and painting are seen as less fit occupations for them than being machine gunners, for example, or baseball players? Why should they live, as most of them do, with the idea that it is, in the main, *their* crippling responsibility to provide for a family when they become grown-up boys? Don't boys and men need liberating, too? Could children's literature be partly to blame for trapping males in a frightful emotional prison and demanding intolerable social expectations of them?

In my own childhood real children were so adversely affected by sexism that a generation later, in a rage, I find myself storming their stories onto paper. For example, in 1957, when my ten-year-old cousin Andrew was taking ballet lessons he was the darling of the ballet teacher. According to her assessment of his talent, Andrew had an exceptional future in dance. One afternoon at the private school he attended, his classmates took his ballet tights out of his schoolbag and threw them into a tree, where they dangled out of reach. He never did ballet again: the maleness of his peers cut him off from realizing his dreams.

I have not called him Andrew when I have written about him. He is instead The Straight Line Wonder (in the book of the same name). He's the one in the Straight Line family who can't keep straight — and I admit to the double entendre in this instance — the one who dances himself into applause and success and lives happily ever after, in spite of his parents' early misgivings about his career. I had to give him, in a book, the future he had been denied in life.

Andrew appears again as my Leo Lipinski, whose father encourages him to follow in his footsteps and enter the world of high finance when clearly Leo's talents lie in the unfinancial world of painting. Whenever Leo paints a new picture, his father's grumpy response is, "Huh. What's the good of that?" It seems to me that parents' expectations of their children's futures remain woefully sexist, so I feel a strong obligation to make it permissible for boys to dance and paint by writing about boys who dance and paint. I write the possibilities into their lives.

Similarly, my old men are allowed to weep in remembrance of things past; my pirates cry; my baby-sitters are leather-wearing teenage boys with punk hair; my heroes in love don't live and love happily ever after; and my male adventurers are led to success by stronger women, without being demeaned by the experience.

By creating these examples I hope I'm liberating males and therefore females, simultaneously. But I hope no one has *quite* realized what I'm doing. I believe that subtlety has conditioned us thus far and that to undo its negative effect writers have to be equally subtle in their approach. I have observed children to be the wisest and most perceptive of critics. They reject quickly as "boring" those teaching-preaching, antisexist stories written by well-meaning, misguided, untalented adults whose propagandist passions far outweigh their artistic ability to tell a good story and tell it well. Laboring the point kills the point of the laboring.

I labor desperately but as quietly as possible. Of the books I have written for children, fourteen are deliberately dominated by main characters who are either girls, female animals, or dynamic elderly women. Three of the twenty-five books have no gender stated at all. In the remaining eight (four of whose titles are unequivocally male: *Tough Boris, Wilfrid Gordon McDonald Partridge, The Secret World of Leo Lipinski*, and *Ben Again*), I have embedded countersexist attitudes intentionally.

I care about what I write, in particular with regard to sexism, because I'm *of* the world, not suspended above it in a valueless, apolitical vacuum. From my point of view there's great danger in writers being cooped up alone, cocooned from the prevailing movements of our time. If we remain aloof from the world we will commit (and are even now committing) crimes of racism, sexism, age-ism, and size-ism without knowing what we have done, thereby perpetuating atrocious opinions and behaviors. Writers and publishers should acknowledge society's fast-changing attitudes toward women, people of color, the elderly, and minorities. Not to be aware is dangerous and arrogant. These Sleeping Uglies of children's literature need to be rudely awoken.

We teachers also need to wake up. It's all too easy to be tricked into a passive acceptance of everything literature presents to us. When we encounter an author writing material that is offensively out-of-date, shouldn't we point it out to our classes? Shouldn't we say, "Hey! This writer must have been fast asleep for the last fifty years to be able to write such rubbish today!"

Of course we *should*, but it's more easily said than done. Although I am both a teacher and a writer who believes she is aware of sexism, I'm still easily tricked into reading blindly and writing badly. Take *With Love, at Christmas*, for instance. I was smugly pleased to have written an Australian book with an old woman as the main protagonist. I was even more smugly pleased to have called the old woman Mrs. Cavallaro, even though it was not an overtly Italian story. It showed I was acknowledging the huge Italian population in Australia, an unusual observation in a national literature whose focus tends to be exclusively and embarrassingly Anglo-Saxon.

For some years *With Love, at Christmas* was published only in the United States; Australian publishers had deemed it too religious. Finally an Australian publisher accepted it, but it needed reillustrating because the Christmas scenes were wintry and our Christmas occurs at the height of summer, so I had the rare opportunity to change the text if I deemed it necessary. I reread it carefully. Imagine my horror at this passage:

> Just before Christmas the husband of one of her neighbours was hurt at work.
>
> "He may never work again," cried the neighbour.
>
> "How shall we live?"

The sexist assumptions in this excerpt are that women are helpless; that they are unable to support a family; that, for them, holding down a paying job outside the home is a great and unusual difficulty; that men are the important breadwinners; and that women are weak. I couldn't believe I had allowed myself to write such drivel: I, whose husband earns less than I do; I, who have held down a paying job outside the home (teaching for twenty-two years) and inside the home *at the same time* (writing for nine years). I was appalled. The passage now reads:

> Just before Christmas, one of her neighbours was hurt at work.
> "She may never work again," cried the husband.
> "Our life will be very hard."

Usually I am more careful, even *trickily* careful, of my portrayal of the female. On the second page of *Koala Lou* a character is described as "tough little Koala Klaws." I know my readers will assume for much of the story that Koala Klaws, being tough, must be male. Much later in the story I write, "It was Koala Klaws who went first. Her climb was a record twenty-two feet in seventy seconds flat." In a quiet way I have, I hope, indicated that it's all right for girls to be tough, and fast, and highly competitive — if that's what they want to be.

Similarly, in *Shoes from Grandpa* Jessie politely and sweetly accepts all the new, girlish winter clothes she has been offered by her extensive family, but the last lines are hers and reveal her character as slightly more tough than expected:

> "You're all so kind, I hate to be mean,
> But please would one of you buy me some jeans?"

The message is not labored, I hope, but it is certainly intentional.

Toughness in girls may need to be encouraged, but I'd like tough boys to have the option *not* to be tough, if necessary. The pirate in *Tough Boris*, in a repetitive series of descriptions, is revealed to be massive, tough, greedy, scruffy, mean, and scary:

> . . . but when his parrot died, he cried and cried.
> All pirates cry, and so do I.

I wrote *Tough Boris* with the deliberate purpose of giving boys permission to cry and to talk about crying. I saw in my mind's eye a father reading it aloud to his son or daughter and wondered, with a writer's wickedness, about the kind of conversation that might develop.

"Do you cry, Dad?"

Pause.

"Yes, I do, as a matter of fact. Sometimes."

"What times? Tell me."

I'd love to be a fly on the wall on such occasions to hear fathers becoming more fully human as they answer these awkward questions.

I also allowed a man to cry in *Wilfrid Gordon McDonald Partridge*. Not only was he a man but he was a very manly man, mad about sports, and cricket in particular:

> He called on Mr. Tippet, who was crazy about cricket.
> "What's a memory?" he asked.
> "It's something that makes you cry, my boy. Something that makes you cry."

Had I not been aware of the endemic sexism in children's books I'm sure I would have made an elderly woman do the crying and Mr. Tippet do the laughing, but I was wide awake at the time, so it's Miss Mitchell who says [about memory], " 'It's something that makes you laugh, my darling. Something that makes you laugh.' " Miss Mitchell is not the one who cries because I don't feel she needs me, as a writer, to give her the permission to cry. Mr. Tippet, on the other hand, does need the permission. So do my boy readers. The message is there, but I've tried to make it scarcely noticeable. I'd hate to be *discovered* as a propagandist, even though that's exactly what I am.

My mother, who is over seventy, is a wonderful propagandist. At twenty-one she scandalized a church congregation by refusing to wear stockings when she was taking an active part in the service — and she was the minister's child. As a missionary she shocked the entire mission, much to my mortification, by wearing shorts. She complains that the danger of surfing at her age is the possibility of losing her false teeth in the waves. She kills snakes without blanching. My wild mother did me the favor of breaking down the social barriers that trap women into narrow paths.

I was lucky. Most girls don't have this array of opportunity spread out before them, so I try to write it into my books, but I hope I am not a shrill propagandist, nor one who is so extreme that she doesn't see the powerful good in so-called feminine attributes such as tenderness and compassion. I poured my love for my own child into the pages of *Koala Lou*, in which the mother is wonderfully loving but very busy. Her abiding love for her eldest, disappointed, uncertain daughter brings anguished tears to my eyes (let alone to those of my readers and listeners) whenever I read the book aloud. It's heartrending to watch children's eyes widen with horror when they realize that Koala Lou has not won that all-important event: "Oh no! Will her mother still love her?" I see them experiencing feelings that reveal deep sensitivities: they aren't hardhearted little toughs, no matter what they say or how they look. Whoever they are, my aim is to make them more able to be tender and kind in a world that aches for these qualities.

Nevertheless, I also make anger possible and acceptable for women and girls. The endless attempt at seeing the other point of view and being reasonable can in the end be counterproductive, it seems to me, and slightly nauseating, in real life as well as in books. A good shouting match will often clear the air more quickly than a cloyingly repressed and self-controlled chat. In *Just Like That* Harriet Harris drives her nice middle-class mother crazy. Her mama reacts with admirable stoicism as disaster after disaster occurs, but finally she cracks:

> "Harriet Harris, that's it, I'VE HAD IT!"
> And she shouted and shouted and shouted while Harriet stood there, just like that.

I want girls to discover from my books that it's legitimate for any mother (not only their own) to lose her temper and to realize that mothers aren't perfect. If they don't have such understandings, impossible fairytale expectations of motherhood are set up that cannot be met.

Both genders have to be allowed to be as real in literature as they are in life. Being tender and kind and funny does not negate being angry or depressed from time to time. All mothers know that! Neither does being tender and kind mean a woman has to be a stay-at-home coward who waits for something to happen. Grandma Poss, in *Possum Magic*, is a quintessentially tender, kind grandmother, but she isn't cowed by the necessity for adventure. She enters into the quest for Hush's visibility with vigor and delight. She is an active, courageous decision maker, not a wan old wimp. She is, in my wildest dreams, the role model for my four-year-old girl readers, seventy years hence; so too are the wild old self-sufficient women who appear in two other books of mine: Daisy O'Grady, the witch in *Guess What?*, and Lily Laceby, the deaf ninety-year-old in *Night Noises*. None of these marvelous women happened by accident onto the page. Sweating at my desk, I created them *on purpose* to give courage to girls in the small hope that the literature I write might make a difference to their lives.

Literature is only part of the cultural media available to our children, but because they learn to read in close relationships with adults, we teachers, parents, and writers have a heaven-sent chance to discuss their constructed world with them, through what they read, and if necessary to rage at the values and question the situations presented. Sexism and the other "isms" may exist in recent literature for children, but none of us should allow any of us to get away with it any longer: to so do is not only to demean ourselves but to sanction unnecessary barriers to the wholeness of our children's future.

Concluding Ideals

In my autobiography, *Dear Mem Fox*, I confessed, among other things, that I would like to be the perfect teacher. Of course it's an *impossible* goal, but in terms of my *Radical Reflections* the following is what I would ask of myself in order to be identified as an excellent and effective teacher of whole language.

First, you ought to be a reader, Mem. If you are not a reader of a wide variety of material from the present and the past, how will you know what to write about or how to write effectively? If you are not a reader, how will you know the books that children might love? If you are not a reader, how will you keep up with the theoretical developments in your field? If you are not a reader, how will you be able to demonstrate to children that you find reading to be a wildly rewarding and highly recommended activity? If you are not a reader, how will you understand the world you live in — the ethnic tensions, the political debates, or the moral values and expectations of society? If you are not a reader, there will be so many gaps in your education and in your feelings about reading you should not *dare* to call yourself a teacher of whole language.

You ought to be a writer, Mem.   If you are not a writer, you will not understand the difficulties of writing. If you are not a writer, you will not know the fears and hopes of the writers you teach. If you are not a writer, you will not be aware of the needs of writers: needs such as a real purpose for writing; a real response to writing; a real knowledge about grammar, spelling, and punctuation to make writing correct. If you are not a writer, you will forget that there are many forms of writing other than stories. If you are not a writer, you will not know writing can be both arduous and tremendous fun. If you are not a writer, you will lack so many first-hand insights into the writing process that you should not *dare* to call yourself a teacher of whole language.

You ought be able to speak and write correctly, Mem.   If you cannot use language correctly, you will lack power in your life; more important, you will be unable to teach children what they need to learn in order to be powerful users of language themselves. If you are unable to write correctly, you should be *ashamed* to call yourself a teacher of whole language.

You ought to be able to create a community of learners, Mem.   If you don't know the students in your classes, as individuals, they will be distanced from you and will be less willing and able to learn. If you don't open up and share who you are with your students, they will not learn to trust you as a teacher and as a fellow human being; this will limit their engagement in class. If you don't create a close-knit community, how will you manage to incorporate the affective to enhance the cognitive in your teaching? If you don't like people and if you don't accept them for what they are, you should not *begin* to call yourself a teacher of whole language.

You should throw out all the unreal language activities you have acquired over the years, Mem.   If you give worksheets to your students, how will they ever learn to write meaningfully and at length? If you rely on basal readers to teach reading, how will your students know that mastering reading is a terrifically worthwhile activity? If you waste time on pointless language activities, you'll have no time to teach real language, in which case you may *never* call yourself a teacher of whole language.

You should remember you're teaching both sexes as well as children with widely differing backgrounds, Mem. If you disregard the girls in your class, you will forget to provide for them literature and language that isn't demeaning to females. If you forget to focus on the girls, you'll constantly be thinking of how to keep the boys interested, to the detriment of the girls' development as people and as users of language. If, with the boys, you focus exclusively on developing so-called male attributes, they won't be able to reach their potential as fully rounded human beings. If you're sexist, racist, or classist, you will be denying important areas of development in the lives of your students. How could you then call yourself a *whole*-language teacher?

You should be an effective speaker and careful listener, Mem.   If you don't listen to your students, they'll think it's all right for them not to listen to you. If you don't model the courtesy of silent attention when others are speaking, how will your students learn that listening is a desirable and difficult skill to master? If you speak with sloppy pronunciation, careless construction, and a limited vocabulary, how will your students be able to observe what it means to be an effective speaker? If you read aloud or speak in a monotone, at an unchanging speed, and with an unvarying volume, how will you capture attention and hold it? How will your students know what it is to be a lively, interesting speaker unless you can demonstrate this ideal for them? If you are so bad a listener and so dull a speaker that your students riot with boredom, can you *really* call yourself a successful teacher of whole language?

You should expect the world from your students, Mem. If you don't have clear expectations, how can your students know what to aim for? If you don't have the highest expectations, how do you know you're not underestimating what your students can do? If you don't reach for the stars, you might be killing potential. If you're not drawing out the best from your students, you're not nearly as good a teacher of whole language as you *think* you are.

Finally, you should remember that every piece of teaching is a piece of research, Mem. When (and not if) you make ghastly mistakes, don't fall into a heap: learn from those mistakes. Teaching, like any art, is an endless cycle of trial and error. If you imagine you will one day have the whole game sewn up, think again and keep thinking. And keep reading and discussing, and changing and experimenting. The best "teacher" you will ever have is careful *reflection* on your own experience as a teacher of whole language in your own classroom.

As I read this demanding list of desirable behaviors, I remember with relief the Robert Louis Stevenson quote "It is better to travel hopefully than to arrive." The Perfect Teacher destination is a long way off, but if we have information, enthusiasm, theories and practices, ideals, and skills stowed away in our backpacks, with the support of one or two cheerful and courageous colleagues along the way, the journey should be very interesting.

I'd like to imagine, as we travel together, that *Radical Reflections* might be a passport to new territory that will excite and challenge us all. We have taken the first step.

Selected Bibliography

Chapter One

Covernton, Jane, ed. *Vile Verse*. Adelaide: Omnibus, 1988.

Mitchell, R., and Taylor, M. "The Integrating Perspective: An Audience-Response Model for Writing." *College English* 41 (1979): 250.

Chapter Four

Adams, Douglas. *The Hitchhiker's Guide to the Galaxy*. New York: Harmony Books, 1980.

Cormier, Robert. *I Am the Cheese*. New York: Pantheon Books, 1977.

Dr. Seuss. *Marvin K. Mooney*. New York: Random House, 1972.

Eastman, P. D. *Are You My Mother?* New York: Random House, 1962.

Hazzard, Shirley. *The Transit of Venus*. New York: Viking Press, 1980.

Hutchins, Pat. *Rosie's Walk*. New York: Macmillan, 1967.

Kelleher, Victor. *Master of the Grove*. London: Viking Kestrel, 1982.

Roughsey, Dick. *The Giant Devil Dingo*. Sydney: Collins, 1974.

Sendak, Maurice. *Where the Wild Things Are*. New York: Harper & Row, 1963.

Smith, Frank. *Essays into Literacy*. Exeter, New Hampshire: Heinemann Educational, 1983.

Townsend, Sue. *The Secret Diary of Adrian Mole, Aged 13¾*. New York: Grove Press, 1986.

Ungerer, Tomi. *The Beast of Monsieur Racine*. New York: Farrar, Straus & Giroux, 1971.

Walker, Alice. *The Color Purple*. New York: Harcourt Brace & Company, 1982.

White, E. B. "The Art of the Essay." *Paris Review* 48 (1969).

Williams, Garth. *The Chicken Book*. New York: Delacorte Press, 1970.

Chapter Five
Byatt, A. S. *Possession*. New York: Random House, 1990.

Chapter Six
Cummings, Phil. *Goodness Gracious!* New York: Orchard Books, 1992.

Chapter Seven
Dr. Seuss. *Hop on Pop*. New York: Random House, 1963.

Henkes, Kevin. *Julius, the Baby of the World*. New York: Greenwillow Books, 1990.

Chapter Eight

Banks, Lynne Reid. *The Indian in the Cupboard.* Garden City, New York: Doubleday, 1980.

Dr. Seuss. *Marvin K. Mooney.* New York: Random House, 1972.

Wild, Margaret. *The Very Best of Friends.* San Diego: Harcourt Brace & Company, 1990.

Chapter Ten

Bemelmans, Ludwig. *Madeline.* New York: Viking Kestrel, 1987.

Jennings, Paul. *Uncanny!* New York: Viking Kestrel, 1991.

——. *Unreal!* New York: Viking Kestrel, 1991.

Terhune, A. P. *Lad: A Dog.* New York: Dutton, 1959.

Books by Mem Fox

Arabella. Illustrated by Vicky Kitanov. New York: Scholastic, 1987.

A Bedtime Story. Illustrated by Sisca Verwoert. Melbourne: Bookshelf, 1987.

A Cat Called Kite. Illustrated by K. Hawley. Gosford, N.S.W., Australia: Ashton Scholastic, 1986.

Dear Mem Fox, I Have Read All Your Books Even the Pathetic Ones: And Other Incidents in the Life of a Children's Book Author. San Diego: Harvest/Harcourt Brace & Company, 1992. Published in Australia in 1990 as *Mem's the Word.*

Feathers and Fools. Illustrated by Lorraine Ellis. Melbourne: Ashwood House, 1989.

Goodnight Sleep Tight. Illustrated by Helen Semmler. Sydney: Century Hutchinson, 1988.

Guess What? Illustrated by Vivienne Goodman. San Diego: Harcourt Brace & Company, 1990.

Hattie and the Fox. Illustrated by Patricia Mullins. New York: Bradbury Press, 1987.

Just Like That. Illustrated by Kilmeny Niland. Sydney: Hodder and Stoughton, 1986.

Koala Lou. Illustrated by Pamela Lofts. San Diego: Harcourt Brace & Company, 1989.

Mem Fox Reads audiocassette. San Diego: Harcourt Brace & Company, 1992.

Memories. Adelaide: Era Publications, 1992.

Night Noises. Illustrated by Terry Denton. San Diego: Harcourt Brace & Company, 1989.

Possum Magic. Illustrated by Julie Vivas. San Diego: Harcourt Brace & Company, 1990.

Sail Away. Illustrated by Pamela Lofts. Gosford, N.S.W., Australia: Ashton Scholastic, 1986.

Shoes from Grandpa. Illustrated by Patricia Mullins. New York: Orchard Books, 1990.

Sophie. Illustrated by Craig Smith. Melbourne: Drakeford/Watts, 1989.

The Straight Line Wonder. Illustrated by Meredith Thomas. Melbourne: Bookshelf, 1987.

Teaching Drama to Young Children. Exeter, New Hampshire: Heinemann, 1986. Published in Australia in 1984 as *How to Teach Drama to Infants Without Really Crying.*

Time for Bed. Illustrated by Jane Dyer. San Diego: Harcourt Brace & Company, 1993.

Wilfrid Gordon McDonald Partridge. Illustrated by Julie Vivas. New York: Kane/Miller, 1985.

With Love, at Christmas. Illustrated by Gary Lippincott. Nashville: Abingdon Press, 1988.

Zoo-Looking. Illustrated by Rodney McRae. Melbourne: Bookshelf, 1986.

The following books are due for U.S. publication within the next few years: *Ben Again, Feathers and Fools,* and *The Secret World of Leo Lipinski.*

Permissions Acknowledgments

Grateful acknowledgment is made to reprint the following:

From *The Chicken Book* by Garth Williams. Copyright 1946, 1970 by Garth Williams. Used by permission of Delacorte Press, a division of Bantam Doubleday Dell Publishing Group, Inc.

Excerpt from *The Very Best of Friends*, text copyright © 1989 by Margaret Wild, reprinted by permission of Harcourt Brace & Company and by permission of Kids Can Press Ltd., Toronto, Canada (Canadian edition).

Excerpt from *Hattie and the Fox* reprinted with the permission of Bradbury Press, an affiliate of Macmillan, Inc., from *Hattie and the Fox* by Mem Fox. Text copyright © 1986 Mem Fox.

Excerpt from *Time for Bed*, text copyright © 1993 by Mem Fox, reprinted by permission of Harcourt Brace & Company.

Excerpt from *Feathers and Fools*, to be published by Harcourt Brace & Company, text copyright © by Mem Fox. Used by permission.